Franklin Wabwoba

Attackability Metrics Model For Secure Service Oriented Architecture

Samuel Mbuguah
Franklin Wabwoba

Attackability Metrics Model For Secure Service Oriented Architecture

LAP LAMBERT Academic Publishing

Impressum / Imprint

Bibliografische Information der Deutschen Nationalbibliothek: Die Deutsche Nationalbibliothek verzeichnet diese Publikation in der Deutschen Nationalbibliografie; detaillierte bibliografische Daten sind im Internet über http://dnb.d-nb.de abrufbar. Alle in diesem Buch genannten Marken und Produktnamen unterliegen warenzeichen-, marken- oder patentrechtlichem Schutz bzw. sind Warenzeichen oder eingetragene Warenzeichen der jeweiligen Inhaber. Die Wiedergabe von Marken, Produktnamen, Gebrauchsnamen, Handelsnamen, Warenbezeichnungen u.s.w. in diesem Werk berechtigt auch ohne besondere Kennzeichnung nicht zu der Annahme, dass solche Namen im Sinne der Warenzeichen- und Markenschutzgesetzgebung als frei zu betrachten wären und daher von jedermann benutzt werden dürften.

Bibliographic information published by the Deutsche Nationalbibliothek: The Deutsche Nationalbibliothek lists this publication in the Deutsche Nationalbibliografie; detailed bibliographic data are available in the Internet at http://dnb.d-nb.de.
Any brand names and product names mentioned in this book are subject to trademark, brand or patent protection and are trademarks or registered trademarks of their respective holders. The use of brand names, product names, common names, trade names, product descriptions etc. even without a particular marking in this work is in no way to be construed to mean that such names may be regarded as unrestricted in respect of trademark and brand protection legislation and could thus be used by anyone.

Coverbild / Cover image: www.ingimage.com

Verlag / Publisher:
LAP LAMBERT Academic Publishing
ist ein Imprint der / is a trademark of
OmniScriptum GmbH & Co. KG
Heinrich-Böcking-Str. 6-8, 66121 Saarbrücken, Deutschland / Germany
Email: info@lap-publishing.com

Herstellung: siehe letzte Seite /
Printed at: see last page
ISBN: 978-3-659-66885-2

DEDICATION
The book is dedicated to Kibabii University College students

ACKNOWLEDGEMENT

We do give thanks to God almighty for giving us the gift of intelligence and perseverance to enable us convert what was initially a dream into reality.

We do sincerely acknowledge the effort of Professor Pang and Dr Waweru for time spent in refocusing the book. Special thanks go to Professor Ogao for taking us through the proposal development. We do appreciate the input of Professor Wanyembi for organizing the seminars to fine tune our ideas. Dr Muchiri's contributions are immeasurable; he really reshaped our thinking and ensured that we published   papers culminating in this book.. He was a gift from God at the right moment in time.

 The National Council of Science of Technology of Kenya gave us research funds and organized a seminar for us, introduced publishing incentives and linked us to other organization that recognized our efforts at publishing. All we can say is a big thank you; you made us know there is a future for research work in Kenya.

Our heartfelt gratitude goes to our wives Beth and Carolyne and our children , Esther, Teresia , Talia, Lecticia, Alvynah, Joshua , Gracious, Daniel and Abigael for their unconditional moral support extended to us at all times. We cannot forget the effort and faith of our parents, Mr. and Mrs. Mbuguah, and Mr and Mrs Dishon who so the need of taking us to school and paying our fees even when there were urgent issues. They started us on this journey that we have travelled longer and further than their wildest imagination. Our brothers and sisters you have been a blessing to us.

Last but no least we cannot forget the Kibabii University College fraternity, it has been a joy being members of this team. Thanks to you all.

Mbuguah SM & Wabwoba F.

TABLE OF CONTENTS

LIST OF TABLES

ACRONYMS AND ABBREVIATIONS

ACOUC -   Accumulated coupling coefficient

ASD -   Average service depth

AVA -   Adaptive variability analysis

CBC -   Count of base classes

CBO -   Coupling between objects

CCC -   Coupling complexity Cohesion

CERT-   Computer Engineering Response Team

CFC -   Control flow complexity

CVE -   Common vulnerabilities and exposures

DCC -   Data call complexity

DIT -   Depth of Inheritance tree

DOS -   Denial of Service

JKUAT-   Jomo Kenyatta University of Agriculture and Technology

LCOM-   Lack of cohesion Method

MCC -   Method call complexity

MDCG -   Method data complexity graph

MMUST-   Masinde Muliro University of Science and Technology

MTTI -   Minimum time to intrusion

OCC -   Object call complexity

RASQ-   Relative Attack surface Quotient

RFC   -   Response for a class

SDLC-   System development life cycle

SLOC-   Source line of Code

TDCC-   Total data call complexity

TMMC-   Total method call complexity

USIE -   User system interaction effect

WMC-   Weighted method complexity

CHAPTER ONE: INTRODUCTION

1.1   Background to the study

The security metrics area poses hard and multi-faceted problems for researchers. Quick resolution is not expected and the likelihood is that not all aspects of the problem are resolvable. Furthermore, only some of those aspects that are resolvable may be able to be done satisfactorily, meeting expectations of repeatability, reproducibility, relevance, timeliness, and cost.   According to Wayne, there are several factors that impede progress in security metrics (Wayne, 2009) such as: The lack of good estimators of system security; the entrenched reliance on subjective, human, qualitative input; the protracted and delusive means commonly used to obtain measurements; the dearth of understanding and insight into the composition of security mechanisms. Wayne identified: formal models of security measurement and metrics; Historical data collection and analysis; artificial intelligence assessment techniques; practicable concrete measurement methods as well Intrinsically Measurable Components as possible research areas.

Issues of security and metrics have been studied for along time, with continuous improvements on metrics and models being carried out, after an analysis of existing models (Wayne, 2009).

Software based system have internal attributes and external attributes. Internal attributes are easy to collect but difficult to interpret while external attributes are hard to collect but easy to interpret (Liu & Traore, 2007). The major internal attribute include coupling, cohesion, complexity. Some external attributes include safety, reliability, maintainability, efficiency, compatibility, portability and attackability. Predictive models allow mapping of hard to interpret internal measurement data into easily interpretable external measurement data.

1

The link between complexity and security is a well-accepted fact in system security engineering (Schroeder et al., 1995; Liu & Traore, 2007). In particular two of these design principles, namely the principle of "psychological acceptability" and the principle of "economy of mechanisms", directly relate to the issue of complexity.

Simplicity is essential in secure systems engineering because complex mechanisms are difficult to build, maintain, and use, and thereby tend to increase security risks. Melton stresses the distinction between psychological complexity and structural complexity. Psychological complexity is based both on system characteristics and human factors, while structural complexity refers to the complexity arising from the software system irrespective of any underlying cognitive considerations (Melton 1990).

The compelling rise of mobile and computer use across the globe is not a passing cloud. Restraints for future growth do exist, while the power, accessibility, affordability of devices makes them an irresistible force in the coming decade. Many people will be using the mobile phones, with advanced capabilities and utilities for banking, surfing, e-commerce, e-governance and communication. It is expected that there will be a tsunami of information insecurity. Software attacks will become more wide spread. It's important to assess the ability of system to withstand attacks at the architectural level rather than at deployment level (Harris, 2010).

From a holistic security engineering point of view, real world systems are often vulnerable to attack despite being protected by elaborate technical safeguards. The weakest point in any security strengthened system is usually the human element; an attack is possible because the designers thought only about their strategy for responding to threats, without anticipating how real users would react. Some of the traits that make people vulnerable to social engineering attacks are: distraction, social compliance, herd mentality, dishonesty, kindness, time pressure, and need/greed (Wilson, 2011).

1.2   The Attackability Problem

The security of a software system depends on both the technical security mechanism and human operator in contact with the system. Thus system designers must not only think about their strategy for responding to threats, but must anticipate how real users would react. For this to happen the system designers require a technical model and social model that could guide them at the architecture stage to predict using internal design metrics whether a software being developed could be susceptible to attack technical or social attack. Yet there appears to be no existing comprehensive predictive attackability model metrics at the design stage to guide the designers. The book aims to enhance the existing predictive attackability metric models by extending the technical attackability metric models, developing a social attackability metric models and finally combining the two to generate the attackability metric which could be used in software system evaluation.

1.3   Conceptual Framework

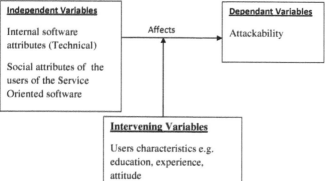

Figure 1. Conceptual Framework (Source: Author)

The conceptual framework has independent variables that consists of the technical attributes that are constituted from software internal attributes that affect the dependant variable attackability. Other independent variables include the social attributes of the system operators that affect the attackability of the software system. Intervening variables may be education, experience and attitude of the subjects. Also other internal software attributes not considered may also compound the relationship.

The aim the book is to provide a model of measurement of attackability that can be used to infer, at architectural design level, the ability of a software system to withstand denial of service attack (DOS) and social attacks.

The specific objectives that will guide the writing of the book are to:

i.   Determine attributes that affect attackability of service oriented software.

ii.   Develop a holistic predictive attackability metrics model for service oriented software systems.

iii. Develop predictive attackability metrics.

iv.   Validate the predictive attackability metrics.

CHAPTER TWO: ATTACKBILITY OF SERVICE ORIENTED ARCHITECTURE SOCIO–TECHNICAL SYSTEMS

2.1 Service Oriented Software

Service oriented software is software based on service oriented architecture (SOA) which is an architectural way of looking at the world, and a way to create a plan called an *SOA* blueprint. From a service-oriented view, a service which forms the basic building block of SOA. It is a way of accessing repeatable business capabilities. SOA services can be snapped together to make other services, and they can be assembled in sequences to make processes (Matsumura et al.,2009).

An SOA service is defined by:

(i)   What the service does for you. A service provides a capability for a service consumer, for example, processing a bank deposit for a customer.

(ii)   How you use it. A service has a specific method for using it, called invocation. It presents a well-defined interface that allows you to access its capability.

However, SOA service does not define the location of service nor how it works. This is because services can be called from anywhere in network and services are opaque Matsumura (2009).

.

Natis (2003) draws a distinction between SOA and Web services. SOA is a software architecture that starts with an interface definition and builds the entire application topology as a topology of interfaces, interface implementations and interface calls. SOA is a relationship of services and service consumers, both software modules large enough to represent a complete business function. Services are software modules that are accessed by name via an interface, typically in a request-reply mode. Service consumers are software that embeds a service interface proxy. While Web services are defined as any software that uses the standards Web Services Description Language (WSDL), Simple Object Access Protocol (SOAP) or Universal Description, Discovery and Integration (UDDI) is a Web service. He says that Web

5

services are about technology specifications, whereas SOA is a software design principle. Notably, Web services' WSDL is an SOA-suitable interface definition standard: this is where Web services and SOA fundamentally connect. In practical use, the ubiquitous Web services standards enhance the mainstream appeal of SOA design (Natis 2003)

2.1.1 The SOA architecture

The architecture of SOA defines the following:

(i)   How to find a service

(ii)   How to make different services interoperate

(iii)   How each service fits into the system-of-services

In SOA, you find services in a registry, you snap them together using composite applications, and you fit them together using a plan called an SOA blueprint.

SOA gains its power by expressing technical capabilities in business terms and allowing business to rapidly recombine them into new solutions. Matsumura (2012 argues that following issues have to be considered when using SOA:

(i)   Coarse granularity describes the size of the components that make up a system. SOA prefers larger components known as business services. These are usually built out of smaller (fine-grained) and pre-existing technical services. This is important because bigger chunks help make SOA services easier for business people to understand, reuse and manage.

(ii)   Interface versus implementation separates what a service does from how it does it. This simplifies the business user's view of SOA focusing on what the service will do rather than the peculiarities of how the technology works under the hood.

(iii)   Contracts define the obligations between the service provider and service consumer. This may include service availability, reliability and performance .This empowers business users to make rational business decisions about which services they can rely on.

6

(iv) Loose coupling is a way of designing services that are more flexible and less dependent on each other. This assists services to couple and recombine. This facilitates faster assembly of business solutions out of off the shelf blocks.

2.1.2 The SOA blueprint

The SOA blueprint should indicate the target state. It should shows the complete picture of what the SOA implementation should look like when it's completed. The blueprint, have a complete list of:

(i) Business services

(ii) Service description requirements

(iii) Service performance metrics

(iv) Interoperability standards

(v) Data schemas

(vi) Policies

(vii) Service discovery and classification requirements

It should also show; SOA infrastructure design which is a map of all the SOA software and hardware components needed, development roadmap which is the step-by-step plan for realizing the complete blueprint and organizational blueprint, the organizational blueprint shows the shape of the final SOA organization (Matsumura 2012).

2.1.3 The Benefits of SOA

According to Natis (2003) the benefits of SOA are:

(i) Incremental development and deployment of business software.

(ii)Reuse of business components in multiple business experiences.

(iii)   Low-cost assembly of some new business processes'

(iv)   Clarity of application topology

He also argues that SOA does not bring these mistakenly attributed benefits:

(i) Simple software engineering.

(ii)Free integration or interoperability.

(iii)   Technology independence.

(iv)   Vendor independence.

(v) The ultimate architecture for the modern enterprise.

The authors concurs with these, using SOA does not mean issues of integration, technology and vendor are non existence but should be considered otherwise the system will require a lot of reengineering to work. The ultimate architecture is still in the distant future.

2.2 Attributes that affect the Attackability of software systems

This section identifies attributes that may contribute to a software systems being successfully attacked. The attributes are software attributes and human operator's attributes/trait that affect software system.

2.2.1 Attack surface

Howard (2003) of Microsoft informally introduced concept of attack surface for the Windows operating system. Pincus and Wing (2004) further elaborated on it and formalized Howard's Relative Attack Surface Quotient (RASQ) measurements for the Windows operating system. He measured the attack surface of seven different versions of the Windows operating system. The results of both the Linux and Windows measurements confirmed perceived beliefs about the relative security of the different versions.

Manadhata & Wing (2005) carried out research on the attack surface, as an improvement of what had been done at Microsoft. Measurement of security, both qualitatively and quantitatively, has been a long standing challenge to the research community, and is of practical importance to industry today. Industry has responded to demands for improvement in software security by increasing effort into creating "more secure" products and services. But how can industry determine if this effort is paying off? Has industry's effort, to make a system more secure paid off? Is the most recent release of a system more secure than the earlier ones? How are the results quantified? To answer these questions they formally defined attackability as cost benefit ratio.

Manadhata & Wing (2005) argued that a system's attack surface is the ways in which the system will be successfully attacked. They defined the attack surface of a system in terms of the system's resources; an attacker uses to attack a system. Intuitively, the more resources available to the attacker, the more exposed the attack surface. The more exposed the attack surface, the more ways the system can be attacked, and hence the more insecure it is.

Critique of the Attack surface
The attack surface measurement method suffers from two major drawbacks: there is no systematic way to identify the relevant subset of system resources that can be used in an attack, and there is no systematic way to identify the set of properties associated with each resource. Howard (2003) used the history of the attacks on Windows to identify twenty attack classes. There was need to have a formal framework for measuring the attack surface without need for prior knowledge of software system. This limitation may mean it is not a good candidate attribute for attackability.

2.2.2 Complexity Measures for Secure Service-Oriented Software Architectures
Liu & Traore (2007) argue that software systems that run in open environments face more and more attacks or intrusions. This situation has brought security concerns into the software development process. Generally, software services are expected not only to satisfy functional requirements but also to be resistant to malicious attacks. Software attackability is defined as the likelihood that an attack on a software system will succeed (Howard, 2003).

Liu & Traore (2007) objective was to develop a quantitative framework for predicting and mitigating software attackability in the early stages of the development process at the architectural level. They explored a quantitative approach for attackability analysis because the use of software metrics as cost effective quality predictors is widely accepted in the software community, both in academia and industry. As argued by Andrew& Whittaker (2005) there are no software systems that are immune to all kinds of attacks. Some software systems may be strongly resistant to one form of software attacks, but seriously vulnerable to another kind. Whittaker believes that some inner features of software products bear directly on the ability of software products to resist against specific forms of software attacks. There is a need to be able to affect these internal features in order to improve software security as an external quality.

Liu & Traore (2007) objective was to use software complexity as one such inner feature. They studied software complexity in the context of service-oriented architectures. They had shown in previous work how the User System Interaction Effect (USIE) paradigm can be used as measurement abstraction to derive various software security metrics (Liu& Traore 2004). They defined a sample metric for service complexity based on the USIE paradigm, and used such metric to bookthe empirical relationship between service complexity and attackability. In their study, they used an open source web based software system as target application and focused on one form of security attack, namely the URL Jumping attack.

It has been argued that in the last several years that a rich body of research has been produced on software complexity (Melton, 1990). At the same time, with the growing interest in software security research there is a consensus that complexity has a negative impact on software security. Liu & Traore (2007) argue that, despite such consensus little effort has been made toward investigating empirically the link between complexity and security in software systems. Existing empirical works on software complexity have targeted for the most part traditional qualities such as correctness, reliability and maintainability, not security.

The link between complexity and security is a well-accepted fact in system security engineering. Such acceptance stems from popular security design principles outlined by Saltzer & Schroedner (1975). In particular two of these design principles, namely the principle of "psychological acceptability" and the principle of "economy of mechanisms", directly relate to the issue of complexity. The principle of "psychological acceptability" states that the introduction of a security mechanism should not make the system more complex than it is without it. The principle of "economy of mechanisms" recommends that system security mechanisms should be kept as simple as possible.

Melton (1990) stresses the distinction between psychological complexity and structural complexity. Psychological complexity is based both on system characteristics and human factors, while structural complexity refers to the complexity arising from the software system irrespective of any underlying cognitive considerations. Although, both forms of complexity affect software security, they limit the scope of their work only to structural complexity. Complexity can be considered as an attribute that affects attackability.

2.2.3 Coupling and Attackability in Software Systems

Liu & Traore (2009) carried out research on the empirical relationship between coupling and attackability in software systems. Their research aim was to develop a quantitative framework for predicting and mitigating software attackability in the early stages of the development process at the architectural level, using a quantitative approach. Prediction models allow the mapping of hard to interpret internal measurement data into easily interpretable external measurement data. Their hypothesis was that attackability increases as the amount of coupling increases in software systems. They investigated the empirical relationship between coupling and attackability by presenting a case bookof a Denial of Service (DoS) attack against a medical record keeping system (MRKS).

Liu& Traore (2009) measured service coupling based on USIE model developed initially to abstract interactions between users and a software system with the objective of highlighting security events and facilitate automated security analysis. Software services can be represented conveniently using the USIE semantics since a software service normally consists of one or more user-system interactions. A USIE model is a graph $U = (N, E, <)$, where N is a set of nodes, E is a set of edges, and $<$ is a partial order relation over E. Coupling could be considered as an attribute that affects attackability.

2.2.4 Complexity, Coupling, and Cohesion Metrics as Early Indicators of, Vulnerabilities

Chowdhury& Zulkermine (2010) carried out a research on the above topic. They argued that security failures in a software system are the mishaps we wish to avoid, but they could not occur without the presence of vulnerabilities in the underlying software. Vulnerability is an instance of a fault in the specification, development, or configuration of software such that its execution can violate an implicit or explicit security policy (Williams, 2008). Vulnerabilities are generally introduced during the development of software.

However, it is difficult to detect vulnerabilities until they manifest themselves as security failures in the operational stage of the software, because security concerns are not always addressed or known sufficiently early during the Software Development Life Cycle (SDLC). It would be useful to know the characteristics of software artifacts that can indicate post-release vulnerabilities – vulnerabilities that are uncovered by at least one security failure during the operational phase of the software. Such indications can help software managers and developers take proactive action against potential vulnerabilities. Chowdhury & Zulkermie (2010) use the term 'vulnerability' to denote post-release vulnerabilities only.

Software metrics are often used to assess the ability of software to achieve a predefined goal. Software metric is a measure of some property of a piece of software. Complexity, coupling, and cohesion (CCC) related metrics can be measured during the software development phases (such as design or coding) and used to evaluate the quality of software. Because high complexity and coupling and low cohesion make understanding, developing, testing, and maintaining software difficult (Fenton & Pfleeger ,1997), these may lead to introduction of vulnerabilities.

Although CCC metrics have been successfully employed to indicate faults in general by other researchers such as Janes (2006) the relationships between these metrics and vulnerabilities have not been extensively investigated. Very few works associate complexity and coupling with vulnerabilities. Shin & William (2008) investigated how vulnerabilities can be inferred from code complexity.

The effect of cohesion on vulnerabilities has never been studied before. In their work, Chowdhury & Zulkermie(2010) explore how vulnerabilities are related to all the three aforementioned aspects - complexity, coupling, and cohesion - both at the code and design level. Their objective being to investigate whether complex, coupled, and non-cohesive software entities are more vulnerable, and, if so, what CCC metrics can be used to indicate vulnerabilities in software? The author opines it would be appropriate to consider relationship between cohesion and attackability.

2.2.5 Attributes that makes People susceptible to Social engineering attacks

Social engineering is defined as an attack in which an attacker uses human interaction to obtain or compromise information about an organization or its computer system [US CERT. 2009]. Cialdini(2009), Lea et al.(2009) and Stajano-Wilson(2009),have all studied scam victims and identified attributes that made them vulnerable to social engineering attacks. They distilled this attributes and the listed them as principles listed Table 1.

Table 1—Scam Victims source (ACM Vol 54)

Principle	Cialdini (1985-2009)	Lea et al, (2009)	Stajano-Wilson (2009)
Distraction		~	X
Social compliance(Authority)	X	-	-
Herd (Social proof)	X		-
Dishonesty			X
Kindness	~		X
Need and greed (Visceral Triggers)	~	X	-
Scarcity (related Time)	X	-	~
Commitment and Consistency	X	-	
Reciprocation	X		~
~ Lists a related Principle			
~Also lists this principle			
X First identified this principle			

Wilson (2011) says that the finding support their thesis that systems involving people can be made secure only if designers understand and acknowledge the inherent vulnerabilities of the human factor.

Their three main contributions were: First hand data not otherwise available in literature; Second they abstracted seven principles; Third they applied the concept to a more general system point of view. They argued that behavioral patterns are not just opportunities for small scale hustlers but also of the human component of any complex system. They suggest that system –security architect should acknowledge the existence of these vulnerabilities as unavoidable consequence of human nature and actively build safeguards to prevent their exploitation (Wilson, 2011).

The authors concurs with these finding and consider the seven attributes as aspect of human nature that may lead to a computers system being attacked based on social engineering These are modeled as social attackability and the corresponding metrics determined which no previous researcher appear to have done.

The authors also consider complexity, cohesion and complexity as software attributes that can lead to technical attackability of software systems. The attack service is not considered due to the fact it requires one to have prior knowledge of software which may not be possible at the architectural design stage.

2.3   Metrics Models for Social Technical Software Systems

This section, discus the existing models that are available relating to software system attackability due to any of the identified attributes/trait. It lists models due to the technical attributes. Social attributes generate social model concerning the identified traits/ attributes and are highlighted. Generic models such as statistical and probability models are also covered. The later two models form basic building blocks from which other models can be synthesized. A model may be defined as a simplified representation of physical system with aim of making it amenable to mathematical analysis **(Distefano et al., 1987).**

2.3.1 Probability models

A probability model is a mathematical representation of a random phenomenon. It is defined by its sample space, events within the sample space, and probabilities associated with each event. The sample space S for a probability model is the set of all possible outcomes (Buechler 2007).

A probability is a numerical value assigned to a given event A. The probability of an event is written $P(A)$, and describes the long-run relative frequency of the event. The first two basic rules of probability are the following(Stroud, 1993):

Rule 1: Any probability P(A) is a number between 0 and 1 ($0 \leq P(A) \leq 1$ 2.1

Rule 2: The probability of the sample space S is equal to 1 (P(S) = 1)   2.2

The classical approach to probability is based on a consideration of the theoretical number of ways in which it is possible for an event A to In general, the following formula describes the calculation of probabilities for equally likely outcomes(Stroud, 1993): If there are k possible outcomes for a phenomenon and each is equally likely, then each individual outcome has probability $1/k$.

The probability of any event A is

$$P(A) = \frac{count\ of\ outcomes\ in\ A}{count\ of\ outcomes\ in\ S} = \frac{count\ of\ outcomes\ in\ A}{k}.$$ 2.3

If two events have no outcomes in common, then they are called disjoint. For example, the possible outcomes of picking a single marble are disjoint: only one color is possible on each pick. The addition of probabilities for disjoint events is the third basic rule of probability (Buechler, 2007).

If there n possible outcomes to a trial, of which x give an event A and y give event B, then provided the events A and B are mutually exclusive

Then $P(AorB) = \frac{x+y}{n} = \frac{x}{n} + \frac{y}{n} = P(A) + P(B)$

If A and B are disjoint, then the probability of either event is the sum of the probabilities   of   the   two   events:
P(A or B) = P(A) + P(B)   2.4

The chance of *any* (one or more) of two or more events occurring is called the union of the events. The probability of the union of disjoint events is the sum of their individual probabilities.

Since an event and its complement together form the entire sample space *S*, the probability of an event A is equal to the probability of the sample space *S*, minus the probability of A^c, as follows(Stroud, 1993):

Rule 4: *The probability that any event A does not occur is $P(A^c) = 1 - P(A)$*   *2.5*

If two events which might occur in succession, such as two flips of a coin are consider. If the outcome of the first event has no effect on the probability of the second event, then the two events are called independent. For two coin flips, the probability of getting a "head" on either flip is 1/2, regardless of the result of the other flip. The fifth basic rule of probability is known as the multiplication rule, and applies only to independent events(Buechler, 2007).

Rule 5: If two events A and B are independent, then the probability of both events is the product of the probabilities for each event: $P(A$ and $B) = P(A)P(B)$…………..2.6

The chance of *all* of two or more events occurring is called the intersection of events. For independent events, the probability of the intersection of two or more events is the product of the probabilities.

2.3.2 Statistical Models

During experimentation we normally have a collection of variables, where each variable is a vector of readings of a specific attribute on the samples in an experiment. Our problem then is: In what way does a variable Y depend on other variables X_1 …………X_n in the study. The solution is a statistical model.

A statistical model defines a mathematical relationship between the X_i 's and Y . The model is a representation of the real Y that aims to replace it as far as possible. At least the model should capture the dependence of Y on the X_i 's (Buechler, 2007).

The dependent variable is the one whose content we are trying to model with other variables, called the independent variables. In any given model there is one response variable (Y above) and there may be many explanatory variables (like X_1…………X_n).

A fundamental aspect of models is the use of model formulas to specify the variables involved in the model and the possible interactions between explanatory variables included in the model. A model formula is input into a function that performs a linear

Regression or ANOVAs, for example, While a model formula bears some resemblance to a mathematical formula, the symbols in the equation mean different things than in algebra.

The goal of a model is to approximate a vector Y with values calculated from the independent variables. Suppose the Y values are $(y_1 \dots y_n)$. The values calculated in the model are called the fitted values and denoted $(\hat{y}_1 \dots \hat{y}_n)$. In general, a "hat" on a quantity means one approximated in a model or through sampling. The goodness of fit is measured with the residuals, $(r_1 \dots r_n)$,

where $r_i = y_i - \hat{y}_i$ 2.7

Two obtain a number that measures the overall size of the residuals we use the residual sum of squares, defined as (Buechler, 2007).

$$R_{ss} = \sum_{i=1}^{n}(y_i - \hat{y}_i)^2$$ 2.8

As R_{SS} decreases $\hat{y}$ becomes a better approximation to y.

The probability and statistical models are basic building blocks for deriving other models. The attackability model will be derived from these traditional models whose mathematical foundation is well set.

2.3.3 Coupling and DOS Attackability Model

Liu & Traore (2009) goal was to identify the relationships between external software attackability and internal software attributes, and then use this information to improve security of software products at the early stage of software development. The specific purpose of the empirical study was to derive a statistic model to demonstrate the correlations between the DOS attackability and coupling measures for software services. In the study there was only one dependent variable and one independent variable, which are DOS attackability and coupling measures respectively. Their experimental hypothesis was simply that "DOS attackability increases as coupling increases" for software services.

The correlation formula for the DOS attackability and the Coupling(*ACOUC*) metrics using statistical regression analysis is presented in this section. Based on the performance of the regression, Liu & Traore(2009) illustrated the strong relationship between the DOS attackability and the corresponding *ACOUC* metrics. Figure 2 shows a scatter plot between DOS attackability and *ACOUC* metrics of the MRKS application.

There is a potential linear relationship between the mean DOS attackability and the corresponding ACOUC metrics, and there is also an increasing trend between the two variables of interest. Therefore, the least-square estimation of the simple linear regression can be conducted. The dependent variable *Y* is the DOS attackability and the software *ACOUC* metrics is the only *X* variable in the regression.

The model being estimated was: $MEANATTACK = a_1 + a_2 ACOUC_t + \epsilon_t$. Where *MEANATTACK* was the variable measuring the mean DOS attackability, *ACOUC* is the *ACOUC* metrics, and ϵ_t is the stochastic error or the random shock for this model; ϵ_t is usually assumed to be normally distributed with mean zero and σ^2 variance. The assumption could be tested by testing the normality of the residual from estimating the model. The normality of ϵ_t also ensures the normality of MEANATTACK, because it is a linear function of the normally distributed variable.

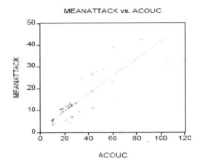

Figure 2 Mean Attack and Accouc. Source(Liu & Traore, 2009)

Liu & Traore(2009) estimation of model was

$$MEANATTACKt = 1.673011 + 0.398372ACCOUCt \qquad 2.9$$

The standard errors, P-values and the corresponding t-statistics of each of the estimators of the coefficients were done. For *ACOUCt,* the p-value was 0, which meant that the variable is significantly different from zero for the sample of data. They then concluded that *ACOUC* is an important explanatory factor for the variable *MEANATTACK* for the sample of data. The R-squared and the adjusted R squared values were both above 70%, which meant that the model explained at least 70% variations in *MEANATTACK*. This indicated that their model performed well in terms of explaining the dependent variable, *MEANATTACK*. F-statistics is another test that way conducted to examine the jointly the significance of the model, the p-value of the test statistics is also 0, which indicated that the variable *ACOUC* was significant.

This model shows the relationship between coupling and attackability. It is the only models that appear to do this. This model will act a seed crystal from which similar models for the other attributes will be constructed. It will be tested in different environment to see whether it holds.

2.3.4 Complexity Model

Object oriented software is a collection of various classes and their relationships. A class further consists of data members and methods. Data members, methods and relationships among classes all contributes to complexity of software. The model introduced by Kaur (2009) determines the class complexity by complexity of all its methods. However, there is no single measure that can measure the complexity of the method, logic of the method, method call, type of method call, data call and relationships, all are constituents of the method complexity. Higher complexity of method's logic makes it difficult to understand and maintain. Higher number of classes involved in a method call and data call is indicator of higher complexity. The relationship through which method or data is called, also contributes to the complexity of method.

Critique of Complexity Model

It is a new complexity model for classes in objects oriented system that computes the class complexity as a sum of complexity of its methods. The proposed model shows that number of method/data calls, type of method/data calls, number of classes involved in method/data calls and control flow of methods highly influence the complexity of class. Higher complexity of class makes it hard to understand and maintain. Comparison with four Chidamber's and Kemerer's (1994) metrics shows that CC is positively correlated with WMC, RFC and CBO. WMC and RFC are highly correlated with CC as compare to CBO. However, the method asserts without proof that that CC is also highly positively correlated with DIT due to the involvement of many classes in method/data calls. Also further empirical research is required using industrial projects to validate the model and to derive more useful results.

The model models complexity but does have an aspect of attackability. But we can move from here knowing that complexity is measureable and extend to attackability.

2.3.5 Five Factor Theory Personality Model

In the final decades of the twentieth century an increasing number of psychologists came to the conclusion that the three factor model was too simple and that 16 factors were too many. In 1990 Paul Costa and Robert McCrae presented their '**Five Factor Theory**' and introduced the associated NEO Personality Inventory. Table 2 depicts the model. Each of these five personality traits describes, relative to other people, the frequency or intensity of a person's feelings, thoughts, or behaviors.

Table 2 Five factor theory Source (Costa &McCrae 1990)

	−							+
Extraversion								
Agreeableness								
Conscientiousness								
Neuroticism								
Openness to Experience								

Everyone possesses all five of these traits to a greater or lesser degree. But there could be significant variation in the degree to which they are both agreeable. In other words, all five personality traits exist on a continuum rather than as attributes that a person does or does not have. Each of the big five personality traits is made up of six facets or sub traits. These can be assessed independently of the trait that they belong to (see Table 3).

2.3.6 HEXACO Personality Model

Kibeom et al.(2008) carried out research on predicting integrity based on HEXACO Model. The model is an improvement on the big five model that has a six-dimension. It has been suggested that the framework may have particular value in organizational settings because of its ability to predict integrity-related outcomes. In the study, they examined the potential value of the HEXACO factor known as Honesty–Humility. First, the empirical distinctness of this construct from the other major dimensions of personality was demonstrated in a high-stakes personnel selection situation. Second, Honesty–Humility was found to predict scores on an integrity test and a business ethical decision making task beyond the level of prediction that was possible using measures based on a traditional Big Five model of personality. This finding was also observed when Honesty–Humility was assessed by familiar acquaintances of the target persons. It was demonstrated that the HEXACO model is applicable within industrial and organizational psychology.

Table 3 Personality traits Source (MacCrae & Costa ,1990)

Personality Trait	Facets
Extraversion	Friendliness
	Gregariousness
	Assertiveness
	Activity-Level
	Excitement-Seeking
	Cheerfulness
Agreeableness	Trust
	Morality
	Altruism
	Cooperation
	Modesty
	Sympathy
Conscientiousness	Self-Efficacy
	Orderliness
	Dutifulness
	Achievement-Striving
	Self-Discipline
	Cautiousness
Neuroticism	Anxiety
	Anger
	Depression
	Self-Consciousness
	Immoderation
	Vulnerability
Openness to experience	Imagination
	ArtisticInterests
	Emotionality
	Adventurousness
	Intellect
	Liberalism

From the literature it can be seen that measurement of the known personality traits is through a percentile scale. This based on self report, questionnaire and peer assessments.

The model indicates how personality traits are measured but none of the social model relates how this may contribute to the attackability of software based system. But they do form the starting ground because we know that models exist to measure personality traits. The authors work is then cut, to move from here and introduce the aspect of attackability.

2.4   Attackability Metrics for Software Systems

Briand et al., (1996) postulates that measurement should be based on Goal Question metrics paradigm developed at University of Maryland. The paradigm states that you have to have a goal of measurement. Then determine the right question to achieve your goal, and then metric is based on this question. The procedure involves the following steps:

    i.   Define experimental goals.
    ii.   State assumptions.
    iii. Formalize relevant measurement concept.
    iv.   Define product abstractions refine properties.
    v.   Define metrics.
    vi.   Experimental validation of metrics.

2.4.1 Attack service Metric

Manadhata and Wing (2005) proposed an Attack service metric to determine whether one version of a system is more secure than another. Rather than measure the absolute security of a system, they measured its relative security: Given two versions, A and B, of a system, they measured whether version A is more secure than version B with respect to their attack surface. They did not use the attack surface metric to determine whether a version of a system is absolutely good or bad, rather to determine whether one version of a system is relatively better or worse than another.

Manadhata et al.,(2005) in introducing this metric they came with the following:

(i)   The entry point and exit point framework to identify the resources that contribute to a system's attack surface.

(ii)   The notion of attackability to determine the attack surface contribution of a resource and the definition of attackability as a cost-benefit ratio to the attacker.

(iii) The notion of attack classes for the convenience in defining the attack surface of a system.

In their prior work, they had defined the attack surface of a system in terms of the system's actions that are externally visible to its users and the system's resources that each action accesses or modifies (Wing, 2004). Every system action can potentially be part of an attack, and hence contributes to attack surface. Similarly, every system resource also contributes to attack surface. Rather than consider all possible system resources, they narrowed their focus on a relevant subset of resource types. Attacks carried out over the years show that certain system resources are more likely to be used in an attack than others. Hence they did not treat all system resources equally.

Manadhata et al.(2005) categorized the system resources into attack classes based on a given set of properties associated with the resources. These properties reflect the attackability of a type of resource, i.e., some types of resource is more likely to be attacked than another type. They used the notion of attack class to distinguish between resources with different attackability. These attack classes together constituted the attack surface of a system. They measured the attack surface of four different versions of the Linux operating system. In their Linux attack surface measurement work, they used the history of attacks on Linux to identify the relevant subset of resources. Similarly, they relied on their knowledge of the Linux operating system to identify the properties of interest. They stated that Howard's (2003) Windows attack surface measurement method suffered from a similar drawback: that there was no systematic way of identifying the attack classes of the Windows operating system.

Manadhata et al.,(2005) work was motivated by the above mentioned difficulties in identifying the attack classes of a system. They defined the attack surface of a system in terms of the attackability of the system's resources. They used the entry point and exit point framework to identify the relevant subset of resources that contribute to the attackability of a system. They determined the attackability of each resource using a cost-benefit ratio to the attacker. They grouped the resources into attack classes based on their attackability. The attackability of these attack classes constituted the attack surface of a system.

2.4.1.1 Other Security Metrics Prior to the Attack surface Metrics

By the year 2005 two measurements approaches were used to determine the security of a system. At the code level, counting the number of bugs found and at the system level, counting the number of times a system version is mentioned in CERT advisories (CERT, 2009), Microsoft Security Bulletins (Microsoft, 2010), MITRE Common Vulnerabilities and Exposures (CVEs) (MITRE, 2010). Both measurements, while useful, were less than satisfactory.

At the code level, many focused on counting and analyzing bugs (Chou, 2001). This is erroneous because the bug detection process may miss some bugs and may raise false positives, and equal importance is given to all bugs, even though some bugs are easier to exploit than others. Many organizations, such as CERT and MITRE, and websites, such as SecurityFocus , track vulnerabilities found in various systems. Counting the number of times a system appears in these bulletins is not an ideal metric because it ignores the specific system configuration that gave rise to the vulnerability, and it does not capture a system's future attackability.

26

Butler (2002) uses multi-attribute risk assessment method to obtain a prioritized list of threats to an organization. The method ranks threats such as scanning, DoS, and password nabbing based on threat frequency and expected outcome. The method focuses on threats to an organization rather than the software systems used in the organization.

Browne et al. (2001) used a mathematical model to reflect the rate at which incidents involving exploits of vulnerability are reported to the CERT. While Beattie et al. (2002) uses a model for finding the appropriate time for applying security patches to a system for optimal uptime. Both of these studies focused on vulnerabilities with respect to their discovery, exploitation and remediation over time, rather than a single system's collective points of vulnerability.

In the area of quantitative modeling of the security of a system, Brocklehurst et al. (1994) measured the operational security of a system by estimating the effort spent by an attacker to cause a security breach in the system and the reward associated with the breach Alves-Foss & Barbosa(1995) used the System Vulnerability Index— obtained by evaluating factors such as system characteristics, potentially neglectful acts and potentially malevolent acts—as a measure of computer system vulnerability.

Voas et al. (1996) proposed the minimum-time-to-intrusion (MTTI) metric based on the predicted period of time before any simulated intrusion can take place. MTTI is a relative metric that allows the users to compare different versions of the same system.

Ortalo et al. (1999) modeled the system as a privilege graph exhibiting its vulnerabilities and estimated the effort spent by the attacker to attack the system successfully, exploiting these vulnerabilities. The estimated effort is a measure of the operational security of the system. These works focused on the vulnerabilities of a system as a measure of its security.

2.4.1.2 Critique of the Attack Surface metric

Manadhata et al.,(2005) method is at a higher level abstraction than the code level, gives implicitly importance to bugs based on ease of exploit. It is at lower level abstraction than the entire system, linking vulnerabilities to specific system configuration. Their attack surface metric is at the design level. The entry points and the exit points of a system act as the entry points of attack on the system. The identification of the entry points and exit points of a system is a step towards the detection and prevention of such attacks. There is need to implement a tool that will uses the entry point and exit point framework to automatically identify the set of entry points and exit points, the set of open channels, and the set of entrusted data items from the source code of a system. The tool could help to automate the attack surface measurement method, identify the entry points and exit points of a system act which act as the entry points for attacks. Hence the tool could be used to identify the parts of the code that could make a system more secure.

Their definition of attackability was based on intuition and experience. There was need to characterize attackability more formally in terms of a model and find out whether the model could be useful threat modeling process (Snyder, 2004). By identifying and ranking threats, they could take appropriate countermeasures, starting with threats that present highest risk. The process, however, lacks a systematic way of performing this step. The users of the threat modeling process rely on their expertise and knowledge of a system to correctly identify the entry points and exit points.

Manadhata et al.,(2005) attack surface measurement method assumes that the source code of a system is available. Prior work on attack surface measurement (Howard, 2003), did not require the source code of a system. This is a short coming of this approach. However their method could be viewed as a first step towards a practical metric for security measurement.

Manadhata et al.(2005) used the notion of the attackability of various resources of the system as a measure of its security. The approach of using vulnerabilities as a measure of security fails to capture a system's future attackability as it misses out on future vulnerabilities. This approach does not take into account a system's design. Their approach focused on a system's design, and hence can be used by system designers and developers to improve the security of a system.

2.4.2 Service Complexity Metrics

Using USIE abstraction (Liu & Traore , 2005), a software system can be represented as a collection of services structured hierarchically where the top service is a composite service representing the application itself. Furthermore, each of the services involved in the hierarchy can be described using a corresponding USIE graph that can be used to derive various metrics. In this case, the measurement targets are the software service entities.

A sample Service complexity metric is defined as follows:

Given a composite service cs and its USIE model UCS $=<$Ncs, Ecs, $<$cs, LCS $>$, the Average Service Depthb(ASD) for UCS is defined as

$$Asd(us) = \sum_{ni \in Ncs} Numberof\ service\ dependence(ni) * Isatomicservice(ni)$$
$$\div \sum_{ni \in Ncs} Isatomicservice(ni)$$

Where

$$Isatomicservice(ni) = \left\{ {1 \atop 0} {\text{if ni is an atomic service node} \atop \text{otherwise}} \right\}. \qquad\qquad 2.10$$

NumOfServiceDependency ni= The number of service nodes depending directly or indirectly on ni (Liu & Traore, 2005).

The USIE model of a composite service explores the inner dependency relationships between atomic services involved. Intuitively, the more inner dependency relationships exist within a composite service, the more structurally complex the composite service ought to be. The ASD metric actually computes the average number of dependency relationships per atomic service node; therefore, high ASD values indicate high degree of dependencies in the service. In other words, ASD metric can be used as a complexity metric for composite services (Liu &Traore, 2005).

2.4.3 Attackability Measure

Liu & Traore (2007) adopt an effort reward approach to assess the external attackability of software services in operational environments. Specifically, they define specific measurements for attack effort and reward with respect to specific software attack. The relative attackability among different software services (or different software applications) facing the same type of attack in identical operational environments can be captured by comparing the attack efforts required under the same reward, or by observing the attack rewards involved under the same effort. Generally, they compute the relative attackability by the $\frac{AttackEffort}{AttackReward}$ ratio 2.11 Specifically for URL jumping attack; they quantify attack effort and reward of the URL jumping attack by defining the following metrics:

(a)   Measure of URL Jumping Attack Effort

Attack Effort service = number of URLs exploited related to the service

(b)   Measure of URL Jumping Attack Reward

$$AttackReward = \begin{cases} 1 \ if \ a \ URL \ jumping \ Vulnerability \ is \ found \ in \ servicei \\ 0 \qquad\qquad\qquad\qquad\qquad\qquad\qquad\qquad otherwise \end{cases}$$

2.12

Specifically, Liu & Traore(2007) define the attack effort for URL jumping attack on a given composite service as the total number of the URLs explored in finding a URL jumping vulnerability and they define the attack reward of URL jumping attack as a binary value which will be set to 1 if there is URL jumping vulnerability in the given composite service and 0 otherwise. Since there is no universal interpretation for the notions of attack effort and reward for URL jumping attack pattern, they defined such measurements based on their own understanding. Traore & Liu (2007) concluded that the URL jumping attackability of a software service and the service's ASD metric value tended to strongly increase in the same directions. As the service ASD metric increased, the service URL jumping attackability increased. Therefore, their hypothesis was supported by the experimental results. The author suggests that experiment should be repeated using different form of attack.

2.4.3.1   Related Security metrics

Voas et al. (1996) proposed a quantitative approach to assess relative security among different versions of the same software system. Their approach, which is named Adaptive Vulnerability Analysis (AVA), exercises software source codes by simulating incoming attacks. A metric is computed by determining whether the simulated attacks undermine the security of the system as defined by the user according to specific application program. AVA applies fault-injection techniques to the source codes of software applications, which makes AVA only applicable in the late stage of software development.

Ortalo et al.(1999) proposed a theoretical model for attackability measurement and associated tools. The theoretical model was based on a description of attack scenarios using the so-called privilege graph. A measurement of the difficulty for attackers to compromise the system is generated from the privilege graph using Markov chains. Global metrics are computed by combining weights assigned by security officers to the arcs of the graph. Their methodology focused primarily on improving system and network security, and does not target individual software applications. Moreover, like many other methodologies, their approach suffers from the fact that they rely to a large extent on subjective primitives.

2.4.3.2 Critique of the Service complexity and Attackability Metrics

Liu & Traore (2007) confirmed that complexity has a negative impact on security. A single case study may not be sufficient to infer a general correlation between the measured structural complexity and the likelihood of successful attack based. Many empirical studies would be required to draw a general conclusion, although their study was a good step in this direction. There was the need to investigate using the methodology of case study the empirical relationship between attackability and many other software security related attributes such as coupling, excess privilege, and internal security mechanism strength. This could allow establishing better understanding of the underpinnings and intricacies of secure software and thereby leading to better products. However attackability metrics was validated and hence it can be used as a measure of attackability.

2.4.4 Service Coupling Metrics

Sharing is common in software systems. Objects and components of a software system are usually shared by different services underlying the software system. Sharing between services naturally involves some form of relationships between them. Liu & Traore (2009) referred to this relationship as Service Coupling. A pair of services may share zero or more components. Some pairs of service may have a stronger coupling relationship than others with respect to specific criteria such as the number of shared components. The degree of coupling can be captured using a coupling coefficient for each coupling relationship between services. Given two services c_i and c_j, we denote the coupling coefficient between the two services by CoupCoefficient (ci,cj). A coupling coefficient should be non negative and equal to zero when there is no coupling. Various metrics can be used to generate the value of the coupling coefficient given the coupling relationship. For instance, a possible coupling coefficient may consist of counting the number of shared persistent entities between two collaborations. This can be derived systematically from the USIE models.

Measure 1. Number of Shared Persistent Entities between two USIE Models: given two USIE models $U1 = (N1, E1, <)$ and $U2 = (N2, E2, <)$, the *Number of Shared Persistent Entities* between $U1$ and $U2$ is (Liu & Traore , 2009)

$$NSPEC(U1, U2) = \sum_{ni=N1 \cap N2} P(n_i),. \qquad 2.13$$

Where $P(n_i) = \begin{cases} 1 & if \ ni \ is \ persitent \ RoleEntity \\ 0 & if \ ni \ is \ a \ transient \ RoleEntity \end{cases}$

By definition, a RoleEntity node is persistent in a USIE model if the corresponding role entity is neither created nor destroyed during the execution of the corresponding service. Otherwise, the RoleEntity node is considered to be transient in the USIE model. Persistent and transient RoleEntity nodes can be identified systematically from a USIE model by analyzing the attributes of the incoming edges of the node, and identifying create and destroy operations. Create and Destroy attributes are denoted by C and D respectively. Using coupling coefficients, they define a measure of the coupling between two sets of services. This measure is referred to as the accumulated coupling coefficient and defined as follows:

Measure 2. Accumulated Coupling Coefficients: Let C denotes the set of services associated with a software system, the Accumulated Coupling Coefficients between two service sets Ci, Cj a subset of C is defined as follows (Liu & Traore , 2009).

$$Accouc(Ci, Cj) = \frac{\sum_{ck \in ci} \sum_{cl \in cj} Coupcoefficient(ck,ci)}{Cardinality(ci) \cdot Cardinality(Cj)}$$

2.14

2.4.5 DOS Attackability Measurement

Due to the diversity of software attacks, it is difficult to capture software attackability universally. Liu & Traore (2009) studied the attackability of different software services with respect to a particular kind of DOS attack. They proposed a reward-effort approach for measuring relative attackability among software services. Their basic strategy consisted of observing the different attack rewards under the same attack effort for different attack scenarios, and then capturing the relative service attackability specifically and objectively by the ratio between reward and effort. For instance, a typical flooding attack aims at either blocking or delaying regular software services by increasing massively workloads on software services. Therefore, the attack effort with respect to this type of DOS attack can be represented by the workload increase, and the attack reward can be defined by the delay in service execution. Liu & Traore(2009) algorithm defines the steps for evaluating the DOS attackability of software services with respect to service availability.

2.4.5.1 Related Works to Service Coupling versus Dos Attackability Metrics

In other researches done such as (Chou,2001) bugs count is used as a measure of software security. Software bugs are collected from either static inspections or testing reports. Using defects count to predict system quality is not reliable as indicated by Fenton & Pfleeger (1997). It is difficult to determine in advance the seriousness of a defect, and in practice, a very small portion of defects in a system might cause almost all the observed security breaches.

In the area of operational security measurement, Brocklehurst et al.(1994), evaluated the ability of a computer system to resist attacks by estimating the attack effort and attack reward. Their approach is based on the analogy between system reliability and security. As time is used to model system reliability, they used attack effort and reward to model system security. A probabilistic model for operation security is suggested in their work. However, subjective interpretation of effort and reward is required in their methodology, which in general is not an easy or precise task. A quantitative metric is computed by determining whether the simulated attacks undermine the security of the system as defined by the user according to specific application program.

2.4.5.2 Critique of Coupling and Dos Attackability Approach

Liu & Traore (2009) admit that even though their coupling metrics are shown to be good explanatory factors for DOS attackability, there might be other independent variables that should have been included in their regression analysis. It is important to investigate the impact of other internal factors such as complexity and cohesion on DOS attackability of software systems. The researcher agrees with and identifies this as gap and proposes to repeat the experiment using the 3C's.

2.4.6 Software Vulnerability and 3C's Metrics

Kaur et al.,(2010) set out to find out whether the **3C's** could be used in predicting the vulnerability of software. They postulate five hypotheses on how vulnerabilities are related to CCC metrics. They argue that if the hypothesized relationships can be empirically validated, this information can be used during the early stages of software development to improve the ultimate security of software products. To validate the hypotheses, they conducted a case based on vulnerability data collected from fifty-two Mozilla Firefox (Mozilla Firefox, 2009) releases developed over a period of four years. They observed that correlation patterns are stable across multiple releases of the software. These observations implied that the metrics could be dependably used as indicators of vulnerabilities.

2.4.6.1 Related Work Vulnerability and 3C's Metrics

Several prior studies such as Janes (2006) have used the Object-Oriented (OO), design-level CCC metrics (commonly known as CK metric suite (Kemerer, 1994) to identify fault-prone modules. In general, the finding is that the OO design metrics can be used to identify the fault-prone modules and predict the number of faults. Research by Shin and others had shown that vulnerable entities have distinctive characteristics from faulty but-non-vulnerable entities in terms of code characteristics (Shin, 2008).

There had been a few attempts at identifying vulnerability-prone modules using code-level complexity metrics. Shin & William hypothesize that "More complex code has more discovered vulnerabilities". This coincides with their one of their hypothesis, H1 (Complexity metrics positively correlates with the number of vulnerabilities). However, they include both design and code complexity metrics, whereas they (Shin & William, 2008) used only code complexity metrics. Their results showed weak correlation between code complexity metrics and vulnerabilities. Hence, their study incorporated some coupling and cohesion metrics which were not considered.

Moreover, Shin and others had only conducted case study on just one component of Mozilla Firefox, whereas they conducted case study on the entire code-base. Liu & Traore (2009) somewhat substantiate the common intuition that service coupling affects Denial of Service (DoS) attackability (the R-squared values of their Logistic

Regression analyses are 70% which means that their model explains about 70% of the variation in attackability). Thus, Liu & Traore (2009) finding complements Chowdhury and Zulkermine experimental findings.

Neuhaus &Zimmerman (2007) had found out that vulnerabilities in Mozilla Firefox components can be inferred from import and function-call patterns. They had identified common patterns of imports (#include in C/C++) and function calls in the vulnerable components using pattern mining techniques.

Chowdhury & Zulkermine (2010) argued that although Neuhaus & Zimmerman findings provide some interesting information about software vulnerabilities, they do not coincide with any of the hypotheses they had formulated. However, they used the vulnerability data in cross checking the accuracy of their vulnerability mapping technique.

Alhazmi et al.,(2007) investigated whether the number of vulnerabilities latent in a software system can be predicted from the already discovered vulnerabilities. They studied the Windows and Red Hat Linux operating systems and modeled the future trends of vulnerability discovery. Their approach has been critiqued as been useful for estimating the effort required to identify and correct undiscovered security vulnerabilities, but cannot identify the location of the vulnerabilities in the source code (Williams, 2008).

2.4.6.2 Critique of the Vulnerability and 3C's Metrics Approach

First is that there are many other factors that can lead to vulnerabilities in software systems, CCC can be some of the major factors to be kept in mind during security assessment of software artifacts, but there is certainly no requirement to limit oneself to this data. Second, vulnerabilities that have not been discovered or publicly announced yet are not used in the study even though that information might have contributed to a more precise analysis. Finally, some conclusions drawn from studying Mozilla Firefox may not apply to other software in different domains.

Chowdhury & Zulkermine (2010) have provided empirical evidence that complex, coupled, and non-cohesive software entities are often less secured. From their extensive empirical study, they found out that complexity, coupling, and lack of cohesion (CCC) metrics positively correlate to the number of vulnerabilities at a statistically significant level. The CCC metrics are consistently correlated to vulnerabilities across several releases of Mozilla Firefox(2009). The stable correlation patterns imply that, once calibrated to a specific project, the metrics can be dependably used to indicate vulnerabilities for new releases. The knowledge gained from their study will help project managers and developers to take proactive actions against potential vulnerabilities in software. However they never constructed vulnerability-prediction models or framework from the CCC metrics. The authors in replicate the experiment based on attackability and not vulnerabilities, for vulnerabilities are retroactive. The models are also be constructed.

2.4.7 Cohesion Measures

This section presents work on module cohesion by researchers such as Stevens et al., (1974).Myers (1975), Yourdon & Constantine (1979), and Nandigam (1995) Bieman & **Kang** (1998). Also, a set of programs is presented in which will be used to illustrate various approaches to computing module cohesion.

2.4.7.1 Definition of Module Cohesion

Stevens et al., (1974) defines module cohesion is an intramodular measure, that measures the strength of functional relatedness among the processing elements within a module. A processing element is defined as a statement, a group of statements, a data definition, or a procedure call; that is, it is any piece of code that accomplishes some work or defines some data. Other terms used in the literature to denote the same concept are module strength, module binding, and module functionality.

The original work by Stevens et al., (1974) Myers (1975), Yourdon & Constantine (1979) on module cohesion resulted in identifying three levels of cohesion. The list has been extended and refined to seven levels of cohesion which have become the de facto standard. These seven levels of cohesion, in the order of increasing cohesion, are: coincidental, logical, temporal, procedural, communicational, sequential, and functional. These levels are defined based on certain associative principles that relate the processing elements in a module.

(a) Coincidental Cohesion

Coincidental cohesion occurs when there is little or no meaningful relationship among the processing elements of a module.

(b) Logical Cohesion

Logical cohesion occurs when the processing elements of a module perform a set of related functions, one of which is selected by the calling module at the time of the invocation of the module.

Temporal Cohesion

Temporal cohesion occurs when the processing elements of a module are executed within the same limited period of time during the execution of the system. Typical examples of temporally cohesive modules are for initialization, termination, housekeeping, and cleanup.

(d) Procedural Cohesion

A set of processing elements are procedurally cohesive if they share a common procedural unit. The common procedural unit may be a loop or a decision structure.

(e) Communicational Cohesion

A set of processing elements are communicational cohesive if they reference the same input data and/or produce the same output data. This is the lowest level where processing elements are related to one another by flow of data rather than flow of control.

(f) Sequential Cohesion

Two processing elements are sequentially cohesive when the output data or results from one processing element serve as input data for the other processing element.

(g) Functional Cohesion

Functional cohesion occurs when all the processing elements of a module contribute to the computation of a single specific result that is returned to the caller of the module.

Table 4 summarizes the original definitions of cohesion levels by listing for each Level of cohesion the associative principle that must hold between a pair of processing elements.

Table 4   Cohesion Associative principles Source (Nandigam, 1995)

Cohesion	Associative Principle
Functional	Both processing elements contribute to a single specific function.
Sequential	The output of one processing element serves as input to the other processing element.
Communicational	Both processing elements reference the same input data and/or output data.
Procedural	Both processing elements belong to the same procedural unit such as a loop or a decision structure.
Temporal	Both processing elements are executed within the same limited time period during the execution of the system.
Logical	One of the processing elements selected at the time of invocation is executed.
Coincidental	None of the other cohesion levels hold between the two processing elements.

2.4.7.2 Cohesion Associative Principle

Any given module is rarely an example of only one associative principle or cohesion. The processing elements of a module may be related by a mixture of the seven levels of cohesion. A given pair of processing elements can be associated by more than one level of cohesion. The steps suggested by Stevens et al., (1974) to determine the cohesion of a module are summarized in Figure 3(a)

Algorithm: *Compute-module-cohesion*

Input: A module's code / design / narrative description

Output: cohesion level of the module

begin

1. Identify the set of processing elements of the module.

2. For each pair of processing elements do

- Identify the set of associative principles in that suitably define the association(s) between the pair.
- The highest level of cohesion corresponding to these principles is the cohesion for the pair.

3. The cohesion of the module is the lowest cohesion that was assigned to any pair of processing elements in step 2.

end

Figure 3(a) The basic steps for computing module cohesion Source (Lakhotia 1993)

A technique commonly suggested by Stevens et al.,(1974) and others to determine the cohesion of a module is by writing an English sentence that accurately describes the function of a module and then examining the sentence structure and keywords in the sentence for an indication of the level of cohesion.

2.4.7.3   Critique of the Cohesion Measures

Nandigam (1995) critiqued the Steven et al., (1974) definition, stating that it is subjective in nature and the associative principles used to distinguish between the various levels of cohesion make it difficult to determine the cohesion of a module precisely. The subjectivity of the measure also leads to problems when studying the effects of module cohesion on attributes of software quality. When a measure is not objective, it is difficult to use the measure for predicting purposes. Nandigam(1995) for his PhD thesis proposed an objective measure for module cohesion, a tool to analyze and determine the cohesion of functions in a C program and validate the proposed measure using controlled and exploratory experiments. They came up with an algorithm to compute model Cohesion Figure 3(b).

Their approach has be critiqued for not including temporal cohesion and functional cohesion in their list of cohesion levels because they thought that temporal relationships between processing elements are difficult to obtain from static analysis of code and that Functional cohesion is only defined on modules with one output.

```
Algorithm Compute-Module-Cohesion
Input:    VDG of module M
Output: Cohesion of module M
begin
  X ← {output variables in M};
  if |X| = 0 then Cohesion ← 'undefined'
    else if |X| = 1 then Cohesion ← 'functional'
          else begin
                cohesion_between_pairs ← {};
                for all x and y in X and x ≠ y do begin
                      cohesion_between_pairs ←
                      cohesion_between_pairs ∪ max{C_i | i ∈ {1..5} ∧ AR_i(x,y) };
                end for;
                if (∀, i ∈ cohesion between pairs ∧ i − coincidental) then
                      Cohesion ← coincidental;
                else
                      Cohesion ← min(cohesion_between_pairs - {coincidental});
                end;
              end
  return Cohesion
end Compute-Module-Cohesion
```

Figure 3(b) Compute - Module Cohesion

Stevens, Myers and Constantine define module cohesion (SMC Cohesion) on an ordinal scale. SMC Cohesion is determined by inspecting the association between all pairs of a module's processing elements. Lakhotia (1993) uses the output variables of a module as the processing elements of SMC Cohesion and defines rules for designating a cohesion level which preserve the intent of SMC Cohesion (Nadagam1995). The associative principles of SMC Cohesion are transformed to relate the output variables based on data dependence relationships.

A variable dependence graph models the control and data dependencies between module variables. The rules for designating a cohesion level are defined using a strict interpretation of the association principles of SMC Cohesion. Because the rules are formal, a tool can automatically perform the classification. However, the technique, as originally defined, can be applied only after the coding stage since it is defined upon the implementation details. SMC Cohesion defines an intuitive notion of the cohesion attribute of design components. Bieman& Otto (1994) used SMC Cohesion as an empirical relation system to help them to define a cohesion measure that satisfies the representation theorem of measurement Fenton 1994) and can be readily automated. Their measure can be applied to both the design and code of a module. It is derived from a design-level view of a module.

2.4.8 Measurements of Personality Traits/Attributes

In this section the research highlights literature review of how the seven personality traits /attributes could be measured based on HEXACO personality and big five factor models.

2.4.8.1 Social compliance

This refers to an inherent personality trait towards obeying authority. In the big five factor this falls as a secondary facet of openness, liberalism. Psychological liberalism refers to a readiness to challenge authority, convention, and traditional values. In its most extreme form, psychological liberalism can even represent outright hostility toward rules, sympathy for law-breakers, and love of ambiguity, chaos, and disorder. Psychological conservatives prefer the security and stability brought by conformity to tradition. Psychological liberalism and conservatism are not identical to political affiliation, but certainly incline individuals toward certain political parties. A self and supervisor report can be designed to measure the trait. The measurement is based on a percentile scale.

2.4.8.2 Honesty/dishonesty

Honesty /dishonesty questions appear more frequently in personality tests .The tests that use these questions are not interested in mitigating circumstances. One is expected agree / disagree with the following types of questions.

i.   Most people are honest by nature.

i.   Most people can be trusted.

ii.   Very few people steal at work.

42

iii.   Teenagers who shoplift should always be punished.

iv.   Most people have never shoplifted as teenagers.

v.   Employees who leave work early without permission are stealing.

vi.   If someone is undercharged in a shop they should tell the cashier.

Others reversed question are:

i.   It is human nature to steal from others.

ii.   The laws against shoplifting are too harsh.

iii.   Most people can not be trusted.

iv.   Teenagers often go through a shoplifting stage.

These are normal tests done and modification of existing test based on the sample questions can be used as the basis for measurement using percentile scale.

2.4.8.3 Time pressure-

Time pressure is a psychological urgency attributed to insufficient time for completing required tasks (Keinan *et al.*, 1987). Time Pressure adversely impacts, decision quality, emotional exhaustion, judgment accuracy, arithmetic performance and promotes exacerbation of negative emotions a questionnaire can be developed that that measures the effects of time pressure on above facets (Chen 2004).

2.4.8. 4   Kindness

A person with a high level of agreeableness in a personality test is usually warm, friendly, and tactful. They generally have an optimistic view of human nature and get along well with others. A person who scores low on agreeableness may put their own interests above those of others. They tend to be distant, unfriendly, and uncooperative. Sample agreeableness items are:

i.   I am interested in people.

ii.   I sympathize with others' feelings.

iii.   I have a soft heart.

iv. I take time out for others.

v. I feel others' emotions.

vi. I make people feel at ease.

vii. I am not really interested in others. (*reversed*)

viii. I insult people. (*reversed*)

ix. I am not interested in other people's problems. (*reversed*)

x. I feel little concern for others. (*reversed*)(Gosling et al. 2003)

Hence kindness can be measured by looking at specific aspect of kindness and using self reports and peer reports as a measure.

2.4.8.5 Greed/Need

Greed refers to that human trait of wanting more and more of something. While need is wanting something urgently and desperately. In either case a questionnaire can be used to assess this attribute. The HEXACO model has an attribute of greed suggesting the use of self reports and observer reports (Kibeom et al, 2008).

2.4.8.6   Herd Mentality

Herd mentality is the characteristics of an individual to follow group thinking. In investments herd mentality causes the expansion and contraction of bubbles, it is necessary to measure it in order to predict bubbles. However, it is impossible to quantify the variable .Instead; consumer confidence was substituted because of its quantifiable nature and correlation with herd mentality. Experiments have been done to demonstrate herd mentality. How ever questionnaires can still be used in assessing herd mentality(Leverton 2003).

2.4.8.7 Distraction

This is when a secondary task obstructs/slows   the user from efficiently and effectively fulfilling the time-critical main task, like driving a car. The main reasons for distraction need to be defined (Scott &Mcinstosh 1999). T¨onnis et al, provided the following types of distractions:

i. Information Overload

ii. Change Blindness

iii.   Perceptual Tunneling

iv.   Cognitive Capture.

Objective measurement tries to find out, how strong the distraction is measured by means of times, distances, failures and successes. The task time is a general indicator for distraction. The time t_{main} is the time spent on the main task. The time $t_{secondary}$ provides the time that is not available for the main task and leads to a decrease in situational awareness. Distraction can be estimated as

$$Ratio = t_{secondary}/t_{main}$$

Additional to the objective measurement methods there are subjective methods. Subjective means asking the user about his personal opinion. Mostly this is done by questionnaires, where NASA-TLX and SWAT are the most common ones. The NASA-TLX is a questionnaire developed by NASA. It provides an overall index for the workload while fulfilling a job. It measures by questioning users for their mental demand, physical demand, temporal demand, performance, effort level, and frustration level and calculates a single value from these results.

Another test is SWAT. It means Subjective Workload Assessment Techniques. It provides an indication for loads for time, mental effort and psychological stress and calculates an index for that.

From the literature review we can conclude any of the social traits can be measured in percentile scale based on self reports, peer/supervisor reports or controlled experiments. The trait measurement is relative as opposed being absolute. The Licket scale is good measure with a weighting of 1 for strongly disagree and a weighting of 5 for strongly agree.

2.5   Metrics Validation

Validation of metrics can be done both theoretically and empirically. Muketha et al.,(2011) says the main goal of theoretical validation is to establish the theoretical soundness of the metrics. Several researches such Fenton et al.,(1998), Weyuker(1988) and Briand et al.,(1998) have studied the metrics for quite some time.

Weyukker(1988) came up with the properties on which to evaluate a metric. First four properties address how sensitive and discriminative the metric is. The fifth property requires that if two classes are combined their metric value should be greater than metric value of each individual class. The sixth property addresses the interaction between two programs/classes. It implies that interaction between program/class A and program/class B is different than interaction between program/class C and program/class B given that interaction between program/class A and program/class C is same. The seventh property requires that a measure be sensitive to statement order within a program/class. The eighth property requires that renaming of variables does not affect the value of a measure. Last property states that the sum of the metric values of a program/class could be less than the metric value of the program/class when considered as a whole. The principles have be critiqued as being ideal for complexity metrics only.

Briand et al.(1998) looked at this and expanded on them by including criteria for evaluating size metrics. Since the proposed attackability metrics are size based then Briand et al.(1998) approach is more applicable in this case.

2.5.1 Representation of Systems and Module

According to Briand et al.(1998), A *system* S will be represented as a pair <E,R>, where E represents the set of elements of S, and R is a binary relation on E ($R \subseteq E \times E$) representing the relationships between S's elements.

Given a system S = <E,R>, a system m = <E_m,R_m> is a *module* of S if and only if $E_m \subseteq E$, $R_m \subseteq E \times E$, and $R_m \subseteq R$. This will be denoted by $m \subseteq S$.

2.5.2 Concept of Size

Briand et al.(1998) says size is recognized as being an important measurement concept and defines size of a system S as function Size(S) that is characterized by the following properties Size.1 - Size.3.

Property *Size.1*: Non-negativity

The size of a system $S = <E,R>$ is non-negative

$$\text{Size(S)} \geq 0 \text{ (Size. I)} \qquad\qquad 2.16$$

Property *Size.2*: Null Value

The size of a system $S = <E,R>$ is null if E is empty

$$E = \varnothing \Rightarrow \text{Size(S)} = 0 \qquad \text{(Size. II)} \qquad\qquad 2.17$$

Property *Size.3*: Module Additivity

The size of a system $S = <E,R>$ is equal to the sum of the sizes of two of its modules $m1 = <Em1,Rm1>$ and $m2 = <Em2,Rm2>$ such that any element of S is an element of either m1 or m2

$$(m1 \subseteq S \text{ and } m2 \subseteq S \text{ and } E = Em1 \cup Em2 \text{ and } Em1 \cap Em2 = \varnothing)$$
$$\Rightarrow \text{Size(S)} = \text{Size(m1)} + \text{Size(m2)} \text{ (Size.III)} \qquad\qquad 2.18$$

The last property Size.3 provides the means to compute the size of a system $S = <E,R>$ from the knowledge of the size of its—disjoint—modules $me = <\{e\},Re>$ whose set of elements is composed of a different element e of E2. $\text{Size(S)} = \sum_{e \in E}$

$$\text{Size(me) (Size. IV)} \qquad\qquad 2.19$$

Therefore, adding elements to a system cannot decrease its size

For each me, it is either $Re=\varnothing$ or $Re=\{<e,e>\}$.

$$(S' = <E',R'> \text{ and } S'' = <E'',R''> \text{ and } E' \subseteq E'') \Rightarrow \text{Size(S')} \leq \text{Size(S'')} \text{ (Size. V)}$$

From the above properties Size.1 - Size.3, it also follows that the size of a system $S = <E,R>$ is not greater than the sum of the sizes of any pair of its modules $m1 = <Em1,Rm1>$ and $m2 = <Em2,Rm2>$, such that any element of S is an element of m1, or m2, or both, i.e.,

$(m1 \subseteq S$ **and** $m2 \subseteq S$ **and** $E = Em1 \cup Em2) \Rightarrow Size(S) \leq Size(m1) + Size(m2)$

(Size.VI)   2.20

The size of a system built by merging such modules cannot be greater than the sum of the sizes of the modules, due to the presence of common elements (lines of code, operators, and class methods). These properties will be used to interrogate the theoretical validity of define metrics.

2.5.3 Empirical validation

The goal of empirically validation of metrics is determine the useful of defined set metrics in industrial setting. It has be argued that there so many metrics yet so few are used to in an industrial environment. This achieved by carrying out experiments to validate the metrics (Muketha, 2011).

2.6 Social Engineering Techniques and Tools

This section looks social engineering techniques, highlights validation of these techniques. It also looks at tools that have been developed to try and automate the detection of insider and social engineering threats to system. The increased dependency on reliable data communication networks has created a need for ever-increasing computer security. Many technological options exist for security in both hardware and software and these implementations pose formidable threats for hackers. However social engineering bypasses the electronic security measures and targets the weakest component of networks - the human users (Kvedar et al.,2010).

Susceptibility to social engineering attacks stems from a lack of formal security management as well as limited education regarding social engineering. Computer security organizations such as SANS are pushing for increased defenses against social engineering (Allen 2004), but until the general business community realizes

48

the threat, very little will be done to implement policies to protect themselves compared to the efforts made to establish electronic safeguards against traditional hacking techniques. Kvedar et al.(2010) carried out some research with the aim of proving the viability of social engineering as a method of network attack, as well as display the need to increase education and implement measures to protect against it.

Computers are designed to provide an unconditional response to a valid instruction set. The same instruction set is used to create different layers of security privileges for different category of users. Social engineering supersedes the explicit nature of machines and focuses on human emotion and tendency. Wetware has been coined to represent the human attached to the computer. Wetware is just as vital to the computer's security as any hardware or software (Allen 2004). It is this wetware that social engineering exploits.

Computers can completely secure information to prevent unauthorized access. This could easily defeat the goal of having information from being readily accessible when needed by privileged users. The goal for a social engineer is to manipulate these authorized users to gain access to privileged information. Aaron Dolan considers social engineering as the "management of human beings in accordance with their place and function in society" (Dolan 2004).

According to Peltier(2006) social engineers prey on humans' desire to be helpful, tendency to trust people, fear of getting in trouble, and willingness to cut corners. They have found out that exploiting weakness in human nature is much easier than exploiting flaws in encrypted software. Instead of physically breaking into bank's safe, it is much easier if one can get the lock pin combination code from a bank worker.

The four phases of social engineering are: information gathering, relationship development, execution, and exploitation (Allen 2004). During the first phase, information gathering, information about company is gathered with the aim of finding weakness that can be exploited and ways of avoiding arrest within the organization. The second phase, relationship development, rapport and trust are developed with contact person within the organization. The third phase is actual execution of the attack where the information is actually exchanged. Finally, the last phase is utilizing information.

Thornburgh (2004) says that an attack is successful only if the target feels compelled to give up the information in spite of their gut instinct. While Manske (2000) says that a successful attack bypasses anything that would be in place to ensure security, including firewalls, secure routers, email, and security guards. This causes unrest and beats the security of encryption.

Winkler and Dealy (1995) provide advice on how to secure a network against social engineering. The list includes not relying on common internal identifiers within an organization, implementing a call back procedure when disclosing protected information, implementing a security awareness program, identifying direct computer support analysts, creating a security alert system, and social engineering to test an organization's security. Dolan (2004) beef up the list by adding; password policies, vulnerability assessments, data classification, acceptable user policy, background checks, termination processes, incident response, physical security, and security awareness training.

Social engineering tactics include impersonation of an important user, third-party authorization, in person attacks, dumpster diving, and shoulder surfing (Peltier, 2006). Dumpster diving involves sifting through a target's waste in search of critical information. However shredders should be used to shred any documents destined to the dustbin. Shoulder surfing is a basic social engineering attack based on attempts to steal passwords and login information by watching a user input the data. This especially true in automated teller machine (ATM) halls, where users do not take precaution to block any other users from seeing them keying their pin numbers. The result is that a lot of clients have lost their funds. My father lost some money from his MPESA account when he unknowingly let a young man know his pin number. The young man , picked his father phone and transferred money from the account to his. However forensic audit helped track down the culprit. Attackers prefer to remain unidentifiable to protect themselves, some tell-tale signs of an individual attempting a social engineering attack include refusal to give contact information, rushing the process, name-dropping, intimidation, small mistakes, and requesting forbidden information or accesses.

Reverse social engineering tact involves creating a situation where the targeted individual actually seeks the attacker for assistance, which provides the attacker with the opportunity to establish trust (Dolan 2004). A common tendency in human nature is for one to feel indebted to their benefactors. Reverse social engineering preys on this tendency. Not only does the target trust the individual, but also feels indebted to the attacker, and will share out information he may not otherwise share out to settle that debt.

In Kenya people have been conned by people pretending to be business men expecting a certain a transaction to go through. After they have developed rapport with the victim they initially ask some money before gradually increasing the amount then finally logging off, leaving the victim high and dry. Another type of fraud executed by Kamiti maximum prisoners is to exploit the greed of their victim. They call the victim informing them that they have won some lottery. They require some information from them, including their MPESA pin numbers. Only for the victim to realize that the conmen have cleared what money they had in their accounts. Once again audit trail by service provider Safaricom located the location of the scam to Kamiti and other prisons in Kenya. This has lead to the company blocking call from Kamiti prison (Safaricom, 2012).

2.6.1 Application of the Techniques a case of CANVAS

Kvedar et al.(2010) goal was to perform a social engineering exercise during the Computer And Network Vulnerability Assessment Simulation (CANVAS) 2010. CANVAS is an annual event in which graduate, undergraduate, and high school students identify vulnerabilities in a simulated networking environment (Collins et al. 2008).In 2010, the students were introduced to a social networking site similar in function to Face book which allowed the students to register users, create public pages and comment on other pages.

During CANVAS, students are assigned to ad hoc teams and must work together to identify and report system vulnerabilities. Many of these weaknesses have been designed into the system to emulate well known system vulnerabilities. The idea was to obtain information about each group's progress in order to identify vulnerabilities in the CANVAS system through social engineering techniques than any single team would have found using standard vulnerability analysis techniques.   In the first phase, Kvedar et al.(2010) study, public resources were used to identify schools participating in CANVAS, their faculty sponsor, contact information, and participating students.

The second phase they initially, tried to establish early communication with the professors attending but they had to abort this approach when they realized most professors were not aware whether their student were participating. They focused relationship building during the day of the actual competition with the students. Prior to the CANVAS event, attackers served as escorts to the visitors in attempt to win trust. The attackers met with the teams on arrival on campus, knowledgeably discussed aspects of the competition, and brought the visitors into the site of the actual competition. The attackers distinguished themselves by dressing in business casual clothes with official university emblems. These clothes were chosen because they were similar to the clothes worn by the faculty members and supported the attackers role as administrators for the competition. This was in support Dolan's (2004) concept of reverse engineering by making the CANVAS participants seek out the attackers in case of need.

In the third phase execution, the attackers were able to convince the competitors that they were acting in an official manner to facilitate the execution of CANVAS. Once the idea was sold, the attackers sought out various teams with the aim of identifying teams that would be suitable target for executing the operation.

At the conclusion of CANVAS each team is required was to submit a report providing an analysis of the network and the vulnerabilities detected as well as offer actions to remedy the vulnerabilities. The attackers also compiled a report that was submitted for judging alongside the reports from the other teams competing without the knowledge of judges or other participating team. A survey was conducted at the end of the day, to bookteams' awareness of social engineering.

2.6.1.1   The Finding of Application Social Engineering (SE) Techniques
The findings are based on Kvedar et al.(2010) experiment. Although the attackers were not the winning team, they able to identify critical vulnerabilities and find specific exploits that could be used to compromise and gain access to the network that the wining team could not.

When students were asked about the role of the attackers during the event, almost 40% of those who answered this question felt that the attacker's role was to gauge progress in the event. Almost 20% viewed the role of the attackers as setting up for the event and another 10% viewed the role of the attackers as to provide hints to teams who needed such help. Faculty who were witnessing the event saw the role of attackers as primarily being responsible for setting up and gauging progress of individual teams. Few viewed the role of the attackers (about 6% students and 2% faculty) as a competition team.

Students, when asked about their willingness to share information, close to 85% reported that they were willing to share information with the attackers as they felt no need to keep such information secret from those who they perceived were part of the event.

When surveyed about whether or not they refrained from releasing information, over 85% of the participants revealed that they did not refrain from sharing the information with the attackers. When asked why they refrained from sharing information with the attackers, several teams commented that they were afraid that another team would overhear information being given to the attackers as opposed to a fear that the attackers would be gathering information about the different teams.

When asked whether or not they had heard of the term social engineering, close to 15% confirmed they did not. 85% of the participants confirmed they did not refrain from releasing information nor did they feel a need to keep such information secret. Over 40% answered that they felt they were not susceptible to social engineering.

At an event where people were focused on network vulnerabilities, information was easily extracted from participants which could have been used for personal benefit. However, teams who identified system vulnerabilities and kept the information to they did better overall, suggesting that they understood the value of such information. Teams who shared their information did not seem to be as concerned with the value of the associated information and were willing to share it with those who they felt had some (albeit weak) rationale for access.

The results from the survey provided some interesting insight into the thought process of those participating. The ratio of people who believed they were susceptible to social engineering to those who did not was almost one to one suggesting that the perceived danger of social engineering is very low. While almost every participant felt comfortable giving the attackers information and most did so, almost half felt they were not susceptible to social engineering, suggesting ignorance to the concept of social engineering. Either one must be addressed through the education of social engineering (Kvedar et al., 2010)

2.6.1.2 Critique of the Findings of CANVAS event

Although this researcher agrees with need social awareness training there is need to provide a measure or metric that managers could use to decide when to offer such training. The background of modern management is the need for objective based management where decisions are based on facts. These facts can only be generated by data objectively collected. This will enable the managers to build a strong case for such training or refresher courses. It can be argued that metrics will be manually collected. What ever the case, this could better than relying on pure subjective judgments. This leads to next question on whether attempts have being made to automate detection of the social engineering attacks.

2.6.2 Ontological Semantic Technology for Detecting Insider Social Engineering

Raskin et al.(2010) describes a computational system tool for detecting unintentional inferences in casual unsolicited and unrestricted verbal output of individuals, potentially responsible for leaked classified information to people with unauthorized access. The tool can also be applied to cases of insider and/or social engineering threats.

The tool can automatically extract hidden semantic information from the casual and unsolicited verbal output of a "person of interest" (POI), both written (blogs, Facebook, Twitter.) and oral (taped conversations), over any period of time. The tool can aid applications in Information Assurance and Security (IAS), where the current approaches are proving to be insufficient. The tool aims to emulate a human investigator inferences mechanism from observations, conversations, and interrogations of a suspect. The easiest case is to find contradicting details about a specific event. A harder case is one without an obvious contradiction (Raskin et al.,2010).

Ontological semantic technogy(OST) utilizes understanding of natural language (NL) text to calculate and extract the information given unintentional by POI. The system does not suffer from fatigue or other human being limitations. Raskin *et al.,* (2001) introduced the theory/ methodology of Ontological Semantics and outlined some directions in which it can serve IAS. OST has undergoing major improvement (Raskin *et al.* 2010) can now be applied in more sophisticated ways. It has advanced beyond adequate representation of the meaning of NL text in Text Meaning Representations (TMRs), to trying to emulate human language understanding as accurately as possible, to inference and reasoning.

At the core of OST are repositories of world and linguistic knowledge, acquired semi-automatically within the approach and used to disambiguate the different meanings of words and sentences and to represent them. These repositories, also known as the static knowledge resources, consist of the ontology, containing language independent concepts and relationships between them; one lexicon per supported language, containing word senses anchored in the language-independent ontology which is used to represent their meaning; and the Proper Name Dictionary (PND), which contains names of people, countries, organizations and their description anchoring them in ontological concepts and interlinking them with other PND entries. A crucial difference between this unintended inference on the one hand and the kind of inferences standards, studied in linguistic pragmatics (Levinson, 1983) should be noted: in conversational implicatures, the speaker deliberately enables the hearer to make a supervised inference, thus, reinterpreting the utterance from its literal meaning to the one intended by the speaker; in figuring out presuppositions, pragmatics focuses only on general, commonly-shared presuppositions.

Raskin et al.,(2010) argue that there has been no known effort to research unintended inference theoretically nor to implement it computationally, let alone applying it to IAS. The lexicon and ontology are used by the Semantic Text Analyzer (STAn), software that produces Text Meaning Representations (TMRs) from the text that it reads. The format of TMRs conforms to the format and interpretation of the ontology. The processed TMRs are entered into InfoStore, a dynamic knowledge resource of OST, from which information is used for further processing and reasoning. The OST ontology is a layered structure of concepts, formed according to a set of rules (Raskin et al.2010)

Each OST lexicon contains senses of words of a natural language that the lexicon describes, mainly in terms of their syntax and semantics. The meaning of each entry is described in the semantic structure (sem-struc) using concepts from the ontology. The syntactic structure (syn-struc) of the entry is governed by the syntactic rules of the natural language described, using a simplified generic notation for lexical functional grammar (Raskin et al.2010). Ambiguous words are defined with as many senses as needed in the following form:

(word (word-sense1)

...

(word-senseN)

)

Each word sense WS is formed according to the following rules:

(WS-PosNo

(**cat**(Pos))

(**synonyms** "WS-PosNo"))

(**anno**(**def** "Str")(**ex** "Str")(**comments** "Str"))

(**syn-struc**((M)(**root**(**$var0**)))(**cat**(Con))(M))

(**sem-struc**(Sem))

)

.

A clear disadvantage and the subject of frequent criticism of similar meaning-based approaches (Sowa 2000) is the considerable upfront investment in the acquisition of the single language independent ontology and a lexicon for each natural language. Ontological Engineering, meaning the creation and maintenance of all resources of an ontological system like OST, is known to be hard (Fridman-Noy & Hafner 1997, Devedzic 2002) and existing guidelines are preliminary, often pertain to controlled vocabularies, not ontology's (Obrst 2007), or are merely concerned with formal and logical consistency (Guarino 2004), rather than with descriptive adequacy.

Application-oriented OST is logically and formally consistent, with its plane of operation being NL meaning. As such, OST generally agrees that its grain size needs to be at the mesoscopic level (Smith 1995) and not have primary commitment to the representation of scientific knowledge. On the other hand, OST resources easily accommodate domain specific information, thus allowing meaning representation and analysis at a finer grain size. The units for capturing the meaning of language in ontology-based resources cannot be statements of commonsense knowledge in formal logic (Lenat, 1990), but, rather, imputed concepts as they exist for human-like linguistic meaning-encoding tasks and as describable by linguistic semantics.

Formal and logical consistency in OST is ensured by checking all acquired and maintained entries against the grammars of the relevant resources and flagging inconsistencies for cleaning or removal. But in addition, the tasks of applications, rather than artificial evaluation criteria used(Raskin *et al.* 2010), are guiding the depth and breadth of the resources and tools. As a result, STAn can adequately interpret the text, sentence by sentence, disambiguating it according to the lexical senses of the words from the lexicon, fully informed by the knowledge of the world captured in the ontology.

2.6.2.1 IAS And Semantic Forensics

Raskin et al.(2010) argues that initially, OST was used to improve IAS with regard to NL files. The result has been a number of applications, some of them NL counterparts of pre-existing applications, others NL extensions and developments of known applications, and still others unique to NL IAS. In the most implemented one, NL watermarking (Atallah *et al.* 2002), a procedure based on a secret large prime number selects certain sentences in a text for water-mark bearing and transforms their TMRs into bit strings that contribute up to 4 bits per sentence to the watermark. The goal of the software is to embed a robust watermark in the hidden semantic meaning of NL text, represented as its TMR in tree structure. The NLP role is to "torture" the TMR tree of the sentence, whose contributing bits do not fit the watermark, so that they do.

As a direct predecessor to the techniques proposed, Raskin *et al.* (2004) described a semantic forensic system based on an earlier version of OST. While other disciplines within cyber forensics explore largely non-textual materials—and those which look at texts, with the above-mentioned exceptions, do not do so linguistically—semantic forensics, uses NLP to identify the clues of deception in NL texts in order to reconstruct the described events as they actually occurred. Like all NLP systems, a semantic forensic NLP system models a human faculty. In this case, it is the human ability to detect deception.

The former ability is a highly desirable but, interestingly, unnecessary precondition for deception detection. The British based school of Linguistic Forensics (Olsson 2004), focuses on bringing linguistic knowledge to the attention of forensic specialists and legal experts. This based on the seminal works by R. Shuy (2005), who pioneered linguistic trial expertise in the 1980s.

Linguistic Forensics was not interested in methodological, let alone technological implementations. Functionality was ultimate goal of semantic forensic NLP but, like all full automation in NLP, it may not be easily attainable. Humans detect lying by analyzing the meaning of what they hear or read and comparing that meaning to other parts of the same discourse, expectations, and to their knowledge of the world.

59

Perhaps the easiest lie to detect is a direct contradiction. The harder type of deception to perceive is by omission. Raskin et al.(2010) gives an example of reading a detailed profile of Howard Dean, one time a leading contender for the Democratic nomination in the US 2004 presidential election, he says that one could notice that the occupation of every single mentioned adult was indicated with the exception of the candidate's father. Another more complicated lie is glossing over an issue.

A new TMR contradicting a previously processed one should lead to an InfoStore flag. The InfoStore component of OST, based on the earlier concept of a fact repository (Nirenburg & Raskin 2004), records the remembered TMR instances. A contradiction will be flagged when some two or more TMR are discovered and compared, and a contradiction, a gap, or some inconsistence is discovered. In the case of the senior Dean's occupation, InfoStore will detect the gap by presenting this information, as given in simplified form as shown in Table 5.

Table5 Example of an InfoStore Result source(Raskin et al.(2010)

exist1

human1

has-family-name "Dean"

has-suffix "III"

has-given-name "Howard"

has-social-role physician1

has-spouse

human2

has-family-name "Dean"

has-given-name "Judy"

has-social-role physician2

has-parent

human3

has-family-name "Dean"

has-suffix "Jr"

has-given-name "Howard"
has-social-role *unknown*

To detect a gloss-over, it is not quite enough to receive a new TMR which contains an event involving a different interaction between these two individuals at the same time. The co-reference module of the analyzer (Nirenburg & Raskin 2004) will have to be able to determine or at least to suspect that these events are indeed one and the same event rather than two consecutive or even parallel events. But a human sleuth does not get such incredibly easy clues most of the time and has to operate on crude proximity and hypothesizing. Also helping him or her is a powerful inferencing module, a must for an NLP system of any reasonable complexity, reinforced by a theory of euphemisms, which must contain typical sets of event types that people lie about, and standardized ways of lying about them.

Raskin *et al.* (2004) outlines the expansion of the ontology by acquiring scripts of complex events, necessary for other higher-end NLP tasks. The main mechanism is simplified to a few sub events, summarized as follows:
1. If a necessary element of a script is missing it is likely to be intentionally omitted.
2. If an element that commonly occurs as part of a script is found in a text, but no other element of it, that is, the script is under instantiated, then the script is likely to be intentionally omitted see   script1.

script1
has-event-as part
and
event1 found in text
event2 not found in text
event3 found in text
script1
has-event-as-part

and

event1 not found in text

event2 <u>found in text</u>

event3 not found in text

Semantic Forensics was an innovative and reasonably sophisticated application of the OST technology deception detection. At that time, however, the technology was still rather limited in its inference abilities, let alone accessing unintended inferences. Semantic forensics could only process what was actually said in the analyzed text, while the unintended inference functionality focuses on the unsaid. Both are perfectly useful and should work cooperatively (Raskin *et al.,* 2010).

2.6.2.2 WD-Inference

This section demonstrates how the unintended inference that is required for catching compromising non-lies is detected and interpreted. Taylor *et al.* (2010) introduced the analysis of a female Facebook user's update, describing her bar experience as, "A white man was hitting on me all night." It occurred to the authors that, without knowing the race of the writer, the update strongly suggests that she is non-white, which was confirmed by an informal poll. What seems to be at work here is that the mention of the race of the man indicates the unexpected and previously unannounced significance of his race. If the writer was white and was typically being hit on by white guys, it is unlikely that she would be interested updating their friends on a common occurrence. The race indication, especially standing alone without any further description, appears to indicate clearly to her readers that his being white is an exception for her.

Raskin et al.(2010) suggests two unequally likely interpretations: either the author usually dates people of her own race, and is therefore non-white, or the author does not date white people and hence unknown to us. He argues the societal stereotype is of people dating within their own race, therefore the former interpretation is more likely. Also for the latter interpretation, some personal knowledge about the writer has to be available to the reader, while the former does not require it, and thus is more accessible. One can refer to the societal stereotype involved in the former interpretation as general knowledge captured in the ontology, and the personal information about a writer/speaker as the personal profile.

An unrelated conversation between two female adult cousins, both professionals, contained a similar example, albeit with a different property involved: My manager wants me to fly economy. Information that is relevant for the inference is that most people fly economy; it is the default for them, and therefore, they are unlikely to make a special mention of it. The fact that the speaker did reveals that her expectations are different. The easiest interpretation is: she usually does not fly economy when traveling on business. To generalize, we assume, throughout the section, that information is revealed by the speaker to the hearer for one of two purposes. One is to add information to the shared knowledge or to contradict or override a default of a known situation or aspect of this situation. Any word in the sentence should either add to the information that the hearer has or adjust the information when necessary" (Taylor *et al.*, 2010). It is when what is modified is an underlying assumed default that we can figure out what the speaker's default is.

As Taylor *et al.* (2010) states, "the computational choice between overwriting and simply adding information depends on the knowledge of what information is implicitly salient for the speaker or whether enough priming has been achieved by the explicitly communicated text, respectively." The salience is either marked in the appropriate ontological concept(s) and/or is calculated by OST.

The simple informal algorithm for calculating the unintended inference of the underlying default is as follows (Raskin et al.2010):

IF in a sentence a non-evaluative property P of a concept
C is filled AND P is not primed, i.e. not appearing in the

63

preceding predetermined low number of TMRs,

THEN the speaker's filler of P for C is set to the

disjunction of all acceptable fillers of P for C, on the

DEFAULT facet, except for the filler appearing in the

TMR.

2.6.2.3 Insider Threat

Insider threat has been actively addressed by the IAS community for at least a decade (Brackney & Anderson 2004, Stamper & Masterson 2002). Mature work on insider threat has focused on the foundational, conceptual, theoretical aspects of the challenge, hoping to develop better countermeasures, which now take the form of policies of prevention of the conditions that are seen as leading to insider threat Willison and Siponen 2009, Farahmand and Spafford 2010).

Insider is a person that has been legitimately empowered with the right to access, represent, or decide about one or more assets of the organization's structure. According to Bishop *et al.* (2008), "there are masqueraders, traitors and naïve insiders." OST can be used to differentiate between traitors and naïve insiders. The most difficult case for exposing an insider traitor is when the perpetrator neither attempts to use any systems which they are not authorized to use nor does anything unusual within their authorized access. They just disclose the information they rightly have to unauthorized parties. The software packages designed to detect unauthorized activities will fail to identify this individual or information that was jeopardized.

Using OST to distinguish between the intentional and unintentional inferences, aims to establish whether the act was "obvious or stealthy". Raskin *et al.* (2010), aim to make further steps towards "the all-embracing knowledge" of "the insider's intent" in future development. They will first consider the malicious insider, called Alice or Bob (A/B), who is unlikely to get caught with some sort of access violations or security leaks. In the best-case scenario for A/B, leave no trace of their activity, other than the fact that the information that only they possessed is now known to unauthorized person(s) without   infiltrating different areas of the system, other than what they normally use. It is normally assumed that there will changes in A/B's behavior/habits/thinking before they got engaged in malicious activity and that these changes should be hidden from others.

Changes in Behavior. Espionage usually requires keeping or preparing materials at home, travelling to signal sites or secret meetings at unusual times and places, change in one's financial status with no corresponding change in job income, and periods of high stress that affects behavior. All of these changes in normal pattern of behavior often come to the attention of other people and must be explained (Farahmand & Spafford 2010).

Raskin *et al.* (2010), assumes the flying economy/business, illustrated using column. Where column S indicates the specific flight by A/B that the conversation addresses; column E shows what class A/B was expected to fly; column F indicates the actual cabin class flown by A/B on this occasion; column U indicates what A/B usually flies, which could be A/B's personal default; and column I sums up the inference. Raskin et al.,(2010) suggest that he general algorithm could be as follows:

If S==Nothing
    U.exp := E
        If U.exp == F
            We are okay, until we find out that U.exp != U
        Else
        S should have been F, if we guessed the values correctly
        if U.exp == U && (U is not widely known)
            trouble
            else adjust U.exp
                we are okay
        Else

65

If E == S //possible trouble

If F == S //at least not lying

If U ==S

Low level of triviality,

but should be checked

Else

OK, according to WD-inference

Else

Real trouble //lied, but why?

If S has lower function value than F

//(in this case, cabin class)

inside threat

Else

Pretending / Social engineering?

Else

//Should be okay

If U != S

Fits the expected behavior

Else

Accommodating group A/B's verbal output can have any significant situation as a topic.

Each situation will replace the attributes and their values characterizing the flight situation with those appropriate to the topic. Raskin et al.(2010) imagined that typical situations and their properties, complete with the incriminating values, are specified in writing for the benefit and training of human counter-espionage experts. It would be no trouble for OST to read, understand, and formalize the salient information from these manuals for use in a computational unintentional inference system of the kind describe here. They also suggest that, in casual conversations about sensitive professional information, it might be possible for OST, to the extent it is possible for human investigators, to tell apart a naïve insider as well as a social engineer from a malicious insider, based on the grain size of the information conveyed.

2.6.3.4 Social Engineering

Social engineering presents a somewhat less varied case than insider threat in spite of an obvious complication, namely, the brevity of a typical hit and thus the small amount of text to analyze for unintentional inference clues. In line with the issue of 'representing' (Bishop *et al.* 2008), Mitnick (2002) refers to it simply as "getting people to do things they wouldn't ordinarily do for a stranger," . In other words, a social engineer called A/B impersonates somebody they are not, normally an employee of the targeted company or its contractor, in order to gain access to their computer network, preferably as a user with appropriate privileges."If someone calls you and uses all the slangy, insider terms of your business, seems conversant in numbering systems unique to your office, and even mirrors your feelings about management and customers, you are going to think that person as is an 'us,' not a 'them'(Long *et al.* 2002). This being the most common and successful approach, typically implemented in no more than two brief conversations, often over the phone, the operation leaves pretty little text on tape.

For the unintended inference mechanism to work, the system needs to have a reasonably representative list of properties with their ranges that can be used in this situation. On top of the information listed in the quotation above, the names of other employees and contacts obtained from a previous encounter are used routinely. The comparison of the conversation with such a property list should raise a flag if the number of explicitly stated defaults exceeds a predefined threshold, which may be as low as two. The recommended lines of defense in the literature include raising the employees' awareness through seminars or posters. The unintended inference mechanism can actually prompt an employee in real time to introduce a value from the range of a property not used by A/B, such as the name of a non-existing fellow employee or a department name, in order to trick A/B into admitting that they know him or it. An experienced social engineer, however, will try to avoid answering the question and to fill the vacuum with asserting information about other properties for which they have already obtained some validating material. Additional distraction can be also used, preferably tied to the original question.

The algorithm of the previous section can be considerably simplified in this case of dealing with only columns E and S.

Given a list L[n] of properties with corresponding values, including the defaults for this group

Count_defaults=0

While conversation lasts

If L[i].S == L[i].E

Count_default ++

If count_default > allowed_default_threshold

Choose unused L[k] and ask a casual question with a

false value of a property

If incorrect response or inconclusive response followed

by a set of (distracting) sentences

Flag, this is a problem

The very simplicity of the algorithm enables the system to analyze the data in real time and to deliver the prompt to the targeted employee during run time (Raskin et al.2010).

2.6.2.5 Critique of OST Tool

The approach demonstrated how an unintentional inference can be used as a line of protection against insider threat and social engineering, given access to an individual's casual and unsolicited verbal output such as blogs, tweets, Facebook updates and conversations with friends, relatives, and colleagues. The unintended inference reaches into text without any apparent contradictions or other visible flags. The approach also illustrated the use of OST to automate this process in a computational system, parts of which have already been implemented while others are conceptualized and algorithmized. The major problem is that based on AI and which relies on central repository of facts and rules. Coming up with facts and rules to covers all cases is a daunting task. Considering that human beings are creative in nature and their strategies evolves with time. However, it's good beginning from which to build on. While it may not flag down all the problems, it can free the human investigator to concentrate on more tricky cases.

2.7 Methodologies for physical penetration testing using social engineering

A penetration test can assess both the IT security and the security of the facility where the IT systems are located. If the penetration tester assesses the IT security, the goal is to obtain or modify marked data located deep in the organizations network. Similarly, in testing the physical security of the location where the IT system is located, the goal of the penetration test is to obtain a specific asset. Physical and digital penetration tests can be complemented with social engineering techniques, where the tester is allowed to use knowledge and help from the employees to mount the attack. In digital penetration tests the resilience of an employee is measured indirectly, by making phone queries or sending fake mail that lure the employee to disclose secret information (Dimkov et al.2010).

Measuring the resilience of an employee against social engineering in a physical penetration test is *direct* and *personal*. When the tester enters the facility of the organization and directly interacts with the employees, she either deceives the employee, trying to obtain more information about the goal, or urges the employee to help her, by letting the tester inside a secure area or giving the tester a credential. The absence of any digital medium in the communication with the employees makes the interaction between the penetration tester and the employee intense, especially if the employee is asked to break company policies. There are three main consequences from personal interaction between the tester and the employee. First, the employee might be stressed by having to choose between helping a colleague and breaking the company policies. Second, the tester might not treat the employee respectfully. Finally, when helping the penetration tester to enter a secure location, the employee loses the trust from the people who reside in the secure location. To avoid ethical and legal implications, organizations may avoid physical penetration testing with social engineering, leaving themselves unaware of attacks where the attacker uses non-digital means to attack the system (Dimkov et al.2010).

Dimkov et al.(2010) attempted to tackle the problem of how to perform a physical penetration test using social engineering in the most respectful manner, while still getting results that lead to improving the security of the organization. They came up with two methodologies for physical penetration tests using social engineering where the goal is to gain possession of a physical asset from the premises of the organization. Both methodologies are designed to reduce the impact of the test on the employees. The methodologies were validated by performing 14 live penetration tests over the two years, where students tried to gain possession of marked laptops placed in buildings of two universities in The Netherlands.

In the computer science literature, there are isolated reports of physical penetration tests using social engineering (Rivlin & Gary. (2006),Stewart & Neil(2009). However, these approaches focus completely on the actions of the penetration tester and do not consider the impact of the test on the employees.

There are a few methodologies for penetration testing. The Open-Source Security Testing Methodology Manual (OSSTMM) provides an extensive list of *what* needs to be checked during a physical penetration test. However, the methodology does not state *how* the testing should be carried out. OSSTMM also does not consider direct interaction between the penetration tester and the employees. Another approach is to use an audit-based methodology for social engineering using direct interaction between the penetration tester and an employee. Since this is an audit-based methodology, the goal is to test *all* employees. Dimkov et al.(2010) methodologies are goal based and focus on the security of a specific physical asset. Employees are considered as an additional mechanism which can be circumvented to achieve the goal, instead of being the goal. The focus is on safety precautions while testing production systems. Since a test can harm the production system, it can cause unforeseeable damages to the organization. The penetration test of the premises of an organization can be seen as a test of a production system.

2.7.1. Requirement for Penetration testing

A penetration test should satisfy five requirements to be useful for the organization S. First, the penetration test needs to be realistic, since it simulates an attack performed by a real adversary. Second, during the test all employees need to be treated with respect. The employees should not be neither stressed, feel uncomfortable nor be at risk during the penetration test, because they might get disappointed with the organization, become disgruntled or even start legal action. Finally, the penetration test should be repeatable, reliable and reportable (Dimkov et al.,2010).These referred to as the R* requirements:

Realistic - employees should act normally, as they would in everyday life.

Respectful - the test is done ethically, by respecting the employees and the mutual trust between employees.

Reliable - the penetration test does not cause productivity loss of employees.

Repeatable - the same test can be performed several times and if the environment does not change, the results should be the same.

Reportable - all actions during the test should be logged and the outcome of the test should be in a form that permits a meaningful and actionable documentation of findings and recommendations.

However, this researcher suggests the requirement should be considered as guide but not rules cast in stone for in practice the requirement is conflicting. In a realistic penetration test;

(i) It might be necessary to deceive an employee, which is not respectful and

(ii) Arbitrary employees might be social engineered to achieve the goal, which is unreliable.

Simulating a penetration requires trade off between the conflicting requirements. If the balance is not achieved, the test might either not fully assess the security of the organization or might harm the employees.

Dimkov et al.(2010) propose two methodologies for conducting a penetration test using social engineering. Both methodologies strike a different balance between the R* requirements and their usage is for different scenarios. Both methodologies assess the security of an organization by testing how difficult it is to gain possession of a pre-defined asset. The methodologies can be used to assess the security of the organization, by revealing two types of security weaknesses: errors in implementation of procedural and physical policies by employees and lack of defined security policies from the management. In the first case, the tests should focus on how well the employees follow the security policies of the organization and how effective the existing physical security controls are. In the second case, the primary goal of the tests is to find and exploit gaps in the existing policies rather than in their implementation.

The environment-focused (EF) methodology, measures the security of the environment where the asset is located. The methodology is suitable for tests where the custodian is not subject of social engineering and is aware of the execution of the test. The custodian focused (CF) methodology is more general, and includes the asset owner in the scope of the test. In this methodology, the owner is not aware of the test. The CF methodology is more realistic, but it is less reliable and respectful to the employees.

2.7.2 Environment-focused method

Dimkov et al.(2010) define the actors , introduce all events that take place during the setup, execution and aftermath of the penetration test, and finally validate the methodology by conducting three penetration tests and present some insights .

Actors: The penetration test involves four different actors.

Security officer - an employee responsible for the security of the organization. The security officer orchestrates the penetration test.

Custodian - an employee in possession of the assets sets up and monitors the penetration test.

Penetration tester - an employee or a contractor trying to gain possession of the asset without being caught.

Employee - person in the organization who has none of the roles above.

As in other penetration testing methodologies, before the start of the test, the security officer sets the scope, the rules of engagement and the goal. The *goal* is gaining physical possession of a marked asset. The scope of the testing provides the penetration tester with a set of locations she is allowed to enter, or processes for adding/removing an employee. The rules of engagement restrict the penetration tester to the tools and means she is allowed to use to reach the target.

The custodian first signs an informed consent form and then sets up the environment, by marking an asset in her possession and installing monitoring equipment. The custodian leaves the asset in her office or an area without people. If the custodian shares an office with other employees, the monitoring equipment should be positioned in such a way that it records only the asset and not the nearby employees. The custodian knows when the test takes place, and has sufficient time to remove/obscure all sensitive and private assets in her room and around the marked asset. Meanwhile, the penetration tester needs to sign the rules of engagement. The OSSTMM methodology provides a comprehensive list of rules of engagement.

The security officer should choose a trustworthy penetration tester and monitor her actions during the execution. A generic script should be defined, which encompasses the stages of all attacks. As an example: enter the building, enter the office, identify and get the asset, and exit the building. For each step in a trace, identify both the mechanisms (if any) that were circumvented and mechanisms that stopped an attack. For failed attacks, the tabulate which mechanisms were circumvented up to the failed action and the mechanism that successfully stopped the attempt. The steps could be:

    i.   Social engineer night pass from an employee.

    ii.   Enter the building early in the morning.

    iii.   Social engineer the cleaning lady to access the office.

    iv.   Cut any protection on the laptop using a bolt cutter.

    v.   Leave the building during office hours.

After the end of the test, the penetration tester prepares a report containing a list of attack traces. Each attack trace contains information of successful or unsuccessful attacks. Based on the report, the security officer debriefs both the custodians and any deceived employees during the test.

Reporting. The attack traces are structured in a report that emphasizes the weak and the strong security mechanisms encountered during the penetration test, structured following 25 techniques for situational crime prevention (Cornish & Clarke, 2003). For different domains there are extensive lists of security mechanisms to enforce the 25 technique .The combination of the attack traces together with the situational crime prevention techniques gives an overview of the circumvented mechanisms (Wilson & Siponen, 2009).

After finding they were deceived by the same organization they work for, the employees might get disappointed or disgruntled. At the end of the test the security officer fully debriefs the custodian and the employees. The debriefing should be done carefully, to maintain or restore the trust between custodian and the employees who helped the tester to gain the asset.

They carried out series physical penetration tests using social engineering on the employees, following the EF methodology. Their finding:

    (i)   Though the penetration tests using qualitative social research might not generalize to other social environments, however, the observations provide an insight of the issues that arose while using the methodology in practice.

    (ii)   The attack scenarios should be flexible. To unplanned event.

    (iii)   The methodology does not respect the trust relationship between the custodian and the employees.

    (iv)   During the penetration test, separating the custodian from the employees is hard.

    (v)   Debriefing proved to be difficult.

2.7.3. Custodian-Focused Method

In the EF methodology, the custodian is aware of the penetration test. The knowledge of the penetration test changes her normal behavior and thus influences the results of the test. Since the asset belongs to the custodian, and the asset is in the office of the custodian, in many environments it is desirable to include the custodian's resistance to social engineering as part of the test. The CF methodology can be seen as a refinement of the EF methodology, based on the experience from the first set of penetration tests. In the CF methodology the custodian is not aware of the test, making the methodology suitable for penetration tests where the goal is to check the overall security of an area including the level of security awareness of the custodian.

There are six actors in the CF methodology.

Security officer - an employee responsible for the security of the organization.

Coordinator - an employee or contractor responsible for the experiment and the behavior of the penetration tester. The coordinator orchestrates the whole penetration test. *Penetration tester* - an employee or contractor who attempts to gain possession of the asset without being caught. *Contact person* - an employee who provides logistic support in the organization and a person to be contacted in case of an emergency. *Custodian* - an employee at whose office the asset resides. The custodian should not be aware of the penetration test. *Employee* - person in the organization who has none of the roles above. The employee should not be aware of the penetration test.

In this methodology, the penetration tester deceives both, the employees and the custodian. Moreover, the contact person also needs to deceive the custodian. The decision which employees need to be debriefed lies with the security officer, and is based on the logs from the penetration tester and the monitoring equipment.

All custodians should be debriefed, because they sign an informed consent at the beginning of the test. However, to preserve the trust between the custodian and the employees, the custodian should not know which employee contributed to the attack. Three elements should be considered before the debriefing.

First, the custodians were deceived by the organization they work for. Second, in case of direct interaction, their privacy might be violated by the logging equipment from the tester. Third, they might be stressed from the penetration test either directly, through interaction with the penetration tester, or indirectly, by finding their asset is gone before the contact person reaches them. The debriefing should focus on the contribution of the custodian in finding the security vulnerabilities in the organization, and the custodian should be rewarded for the participation.

The method was validated using eleven penetration tests with the custodian focused methodology. Their finding were

(i)   It should be specified in advance which information the penetration tester is allowed to use.

(ii)   Panic situations need to be taken into consideration in the termination conditions.

(iii)   The penetration test cannot be repeated many times.

2.7.4 Evaluation of the two methodologies

Table 5 shows an evaluation of the two methodologies.

Table 5 Environment and Custodian Methodologies (Dimkov et al.(2010))

Criteria	Environment Focused	Custodian Focused
Reliable	The result of the penetration test will not affect the productivity of the custodian or any other employees.	The productivity of the custodian is only that may be affected.
Repeatable	Questionable	Questionable
reportable	completely covers all information	completely covers all information
respectful	Not completely respectful	Not completely respectful
Realistic	Not realistic	realistic

2.7.5 Critique of the two methodologies

The main critique about the two methodologies is that not respectful of person. Hence the methodologies are unethical. However, it has be argued that for tests its not possible to execute them without deception. In this respect Finn (1995) list four justifications that need to satisfy for deception to be acceptable these are:

(i)   The assessment cannot be performed without the use of deception.

(ii)   The knowledge obtained from the assessment has important value.

(iii)   The test involves no more than minimal risk and does not violate the rights and the welfare of the individual.

(iv)   Where appropriate, the subjects are provided with relevant information about the assessment after participating in the test.

Physical penetration testing using social engineering can never be completely respectful because it is based on deception. However, the deception in both methodologies could be justifiable.

Securing an organization requires penetration testing on the IT security, the physical security of the location where the IT systems are situated, as well as evaluating the security awareness of the employees who work with these systems.. The two methodologies presented for penetration testing used social engineering, it could be interesting to find control experiment that did not use social engineering. The custodian-focused methodology improves on the environment-focused methodology in many aspects. However, the environment-focused methodology is more reliable, does not deceive the custodian and fully debriefs all actors in the test. The researches concurs with the conclusion that physical penetration tests using social engineering can reduce the impact on employees in the organization, and provide meaningful and useful information on the security posture of the organization. He also agrees that the need to:

(i)   Investigate the effect of the perceived importance of the asset on the results of the test.

(ii)   Investigate the aspect of *safety* for both the employees and the testers.

2.7.5 Algorithm

An algorithm is a method or a process followed to solve a problem. If the problem is viewed as a function, then an algorithm is an implementation for the function that transforms an input to the corresponding output. A problem can be solved by many different algorithms. A given algorithm solves only one problem (Shaffer 2011).

By definition, something can only be called an algorithm if it has all of the following properties (Shaffer 2011).

i.   It must be correct. In other words, it must compute the desired function, converting each input to the correct output.

ii.   It is composed of a series of concrete steps. Concrete means that the action described by that step is completely understood and doable by the person or machine that must perform the algorithm. Each step must also be doable in a finite amount of time.

iii.   There can be no ambiguity as to which step will be performed next. Often it is the next step of the algorithm description.

iv.   It must be composed of a finite number of steps.

v.   It must terminate. In other words, it may not go into an infinite loop.

It important to write and algorithm to automate any metrics so defined.

2.9 Summary

This section identified gaps that form the bases of the next chapters. A summary is listed in Table 6.The emphasis is on relevant models and their short coming, technical attribute and their relationship to attackability. The social attributes identified are included as well as their models that show the relationships between these attributes and social attackability of socio- technical system. The lists include names of the authors their contribution and gaps in their research (See Table 6)

Wayne also identifies formal security model as suitable research area. The author concentrates on attackability and the 3'C as opposed vulnerability as done by Chowdhury and Zulkermine. The authors agree with the two that undetected vulnerabilities can not be used to predict future vulnerabilities. Also, a lot of work has been done on vulnerabilities and little on attackability, hence the motivation for this study.

The book considers CCC and establishes a correlation among them and attackability. Establishes a model for each as far as DOS attack is concerned. Combines the three

Table 6 –Summary source (Author)

Authors	Existing metrics models-contribution	Limitations
Micheal Howard (2003)	Introduced the notion of attack surface.	Lack of a systematic way of identifying attack surface, resources required and based on prior knowledge
Manadhata et al.(2005)	Introduced the (i) entry exit point framework for identifying the resources and attack surface. (ii) the concept of attackability as a cost benefit ratio (iii) the notion of attack surface classes for defining the attack surface.	The definition was based on intuition and hence the need to characterize it in a formal model.
Traore and Liu (2007)	Established a correlation between attackability and complexity using a URL jumping attack.	Did not model the relationship and did not test it with any other type of attack
Liu & Traore.(2009)	Established a correlation between attackability and coupling using DOS attack Modeled the relationship	Did not model for any other internal attributes such as complexity and cohesion.
Chowdhury and Zulkermie (2010)	Established correlation between CCC and vulnerability.	Did not model for the relationships. He used data mined from known vulnerabilities. Data from unknown vulnerabilities cannot be used to predict the future.
Ciadini, Lea et al. and Sajano-Wilson (2011)	Identified the principles that scam victims respond to and hypothesized that same principles apply to software systems under social engineering attack.	They did not attempt to model the same.

models to generate a technical attackability model from which a technical attackability metric is derived.

The human traits are also modeled to assist in evaluation of social attacks and combined with the technical metrics model to produce a holistic predictive attackability model. A simplified conceptual model can be found in section 1.3. The author in July 2012 published a detailed conceptual model of the proposed holistic predicative attackability metric model (Mbuguah et al. 2012)

It uses the definition of attackability as.

Attackability = r/e where

$$e= \sum \frac{WS_{attack}}{WS} \; and \; r = \sum \frac{TS_{attack}}{TS}$$

The operation definition of terms social aspects terms is used are defined in Table 7(a)

Table 7(a) – Variables Source (Author)

Trait	Variables	Description
Distractions	DIST	The degree to which a person can concentrate on issue as to be oblivious of the environment
Social compliance,	SOCOM	The respect to authority, meaning that reference to authority can cause one bend or breaks rules
herd mentality	HERD	The fact that everyone else appear to be doing something others follow them even its illegal
dishonesty	DISHON	Doing something dishonesty and being held captive to guilty as to what one may not normally do.
Kindness	KIND	The tendency to be kind to others can be exploited as to force one to trust con artist
time pressure	TIMEP	Being pressured to make decision in hurry making one take decision without consulting or thinking through hence being subject to manipulations
need/greed	NEED	The desire to have something or greed may force one into being compromised

CHAPTER THREE: THE HOLISTIC PREDICTIVE ATTACKABILITY METRICS (PAM) MODEL DEVELOPMENT

3.1 Introduction

One of the objectives was to develop a holistic predictive attackability metric model, This chapter illustrates the procedure followed in developing the model. A model is an attempt to approximate a physical system based on some assumptions. Modeling is necessary to convert a system into a form amenable to mathematical analysis. From literature survey seven social attributes (Dishonest Distraction, Kindness, Greedy, Time Pressure, Social compliance and, Herd mentality) and three technical attributes (Complexity, Cohesion & Coupling) were identified. The authors postulated that each had a positive correlation with mean attackability of the system. However, for technical attributes, since a strong cohesion is normally equated to a weak coupling the two were considered to work in opposition. The Holistic predictive Attackability metrics model was developed in three stages. Stage one the technical model, stage two social model and stage three the holistic model.

3.2 Technical Attackability Model

The attributes are 3C's , we model for each. The coupling model had been model as a statistical model with relationship of(see 2.4.3).

$$\text{MeanattackCoup} = 1.673 + 0.4\text{Coupt.} \qquad 3.1$$

This model is assumed to hold in this case.

MeanAttackComp due to Complexity is considered to have positive linear relationship such that it can be model as statistical model. With Meanattackability being considered the dependant variable and complexity the independent variable. The model equation will then be

$$\text{MeanttackComp} = A0 + A_1\text{Compt} + \epsilon_1 \qquad 3.2$$

Where A0 is the point at which it cuts the Y-Axis assuming linear relationship with meanAttackability being on the Y-Axis and Complexity being on X-axis. ϵ_1 is considered an error value to be determined experimentally. While A1 represents the gradient.

Cohesion has positive relation with meanattackability however in opposite direction to that of coupling. The relationship between weak cohesion and strong cohesion is not linear. For the sake of the model it will be considered non linear and represented by a quadratic function but this will be determined experimentally

$$\text{ManattackCohen} = B_0 + B_1\text{Cohent} + B_2\text{Cohen}^2t + \epsilon_2 \qquad\qquad 3.3$$

Where ϵ_2, is the random error, Bo the point at which it cuts the Y –axis. While B_2 and B_1 are the coefficients of cohen^2 and Cohen terms respectively. Figure 4(a) shows the Technical model

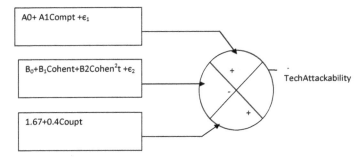

Figure 4(a) Technical attackability Model Source(Author)

$$\text{MeanTechAttackability} = (1.673 + 0.4\text{Coupt.}) + (A_0 + A_1\text{Compt} + \epsilon_1) - (B_0 + B_1\text{Cohent} + B_2\text{Cohen}^2t + \epsilon_2). \qquad 3.4$$

3.3 The Social attackability model

From the discussion in section 2.4.1 then the social attributes can form a probability model whose sample space is

S = {Dishonest(Dishon), Distraction(Dist),Kindness(Kind),Greedy/need(greed), Time Pressure(Timep), Social compliance(Socom) ,Herd mentality(Herd)

S={Dishon, Dist, Kind, Greed, TimeP, Socom, Herd}   3.5

An event A, being a subset of sample space such as considering Dishon only.

For the model we require determine the frequency of occurrence of an event A. This will be determined from Questionnaire tool that is used in data collection. Using SPSS frequency descriptive analysis will be determined. Using five scale Likert scale the participants will be asked rate in scale comprising of {Strongly agree, Agree, Do not Know, disagree and strongly disagree) whether any of traits in sample space contribute to Social attackability of system. This scale will then quantified as

{5, 4, 3, 2, 1}.Assuming that the number of participant is N then

Count of outcome in S, k=5N.

Count of outcome in A , j= (5*(no of strongly agree)+4*(no of agree) +3*(no of DNK) + 2*(no of disagree) +1*(Strongly disagree)

$P(A) = j/k$ 3.6

In the model we shall have seven disjoint events and rule 4(section 2.4) will apply . P(S)={P(Dishon), P(Dist), P(Kind), P(Greed), P(TimeP), P(Socom), (P)Herd}

For the whole model to be predictive then each part should also be predictive, for this to happen then we assume each trait in the sample space is equally likely to occur since the sample space is seven then

$P(A) = 1/7$ 3.7

But we also have Probability(Union) duo to union of individual probabilities.

Hence this two probabilities can be considered sequential and independent and rule five applies(section 2.4.1). Figure 4(b) shows the social model

Predictive probability (Intersection)= 1/7*P(union)

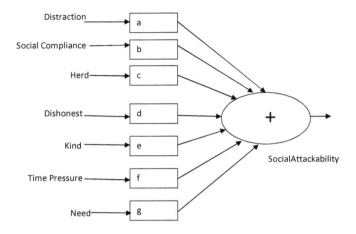

Figure 4(b)   Social attackability Model source (Author)

MeanSocialAttack= (aDist+bSocom+cHerd+dDishon+eKind+fTimeP+gNeed) 4.9

3.4 The Holistic Predictive model Attackability Metric Model

Figure 4(c) shows the model which constitutes two main blocks. The upper block illustrates Technical attackability metric model derived from the coupling, cohesion and complexity. The lower block illustrates the social attackability metric model. The seven human traits are modeled and used to derive the mean social attackability metric which is combined with Technical attackability metric to generate the system holistic predictive attackability metrics model.

The upper block indicates that the coupling versus attackability has been modeled. No modeling on complexity and cohesion has been done. The researchers propose to model for the two and then combine with coupling model to generate the Technical predictive model to produce a holistic attackability model, expected to be a statistical

86

model. Hence they can all be combined to produce a technical complexity model and metric.

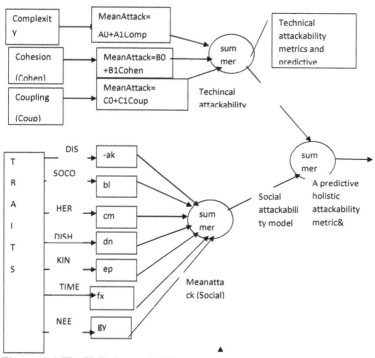

Figure 4(c) The Holistic attackability model source (Mbugual et al., 2012)

It can be assumed that each of the seven attributes occur in equal measure. If this be the case the factor labeled "k" to "y" will be 1/7.This can be verified by carrying out a research through, questionnaires, interviews, penetration tests and observations. If this is not the case then data collected can then be used to determine the frequency of occurrence of each which will be used to determine the factors "a" to "g". It can also be assumed that each of the trait contribute in equal measure to social attackability. This may not be the case the variables "a" to "g" assessment of weighting of the probable contribution to each them. It is assumed that the model of each will be probability and all of them can be combined to generate a social attackability model and hence metric.

To generate a holistic predictive model and metric the technical model and social model should be combined to produce a metric. In the ideal case the metric should be numerical value. But there could be issues on whether this is justifiable. The researcher proposes to avoid this by proposing that the final metric $M = mT + nS$ where small m represents the technical metric and n represents social metric.

3.5 Summary
The process of the model development has been explained in this chapter. The holistic predictive attackability models synthesized from a technical model which is a statistical model and a social model which is a probability model. Technical model is synthesized from three statistical models of complexity, coupling and cohesion each versus attackability. The social model is union of probability models of each of seven attributes and attackability.

CHAPTER FOUR: ATTACKABILITY METRICS

4.1 Introduction

This section describes defines the metrics as per model (Figure 4c). The theoretical validity of both social attackability metrics illustrated. How to measure attackability was defined in equation 4.0 as MeanAttackability = r/e where

$$e = \sum \frac{Ws - Wattack}{Ws} \quad \text{and } r = \sum \frac{Ts - Tattack}{Ts} \qquad 4.0$$

4.2 Technical attackability metrics

From the technical model(section 4.2) the following are defined as the relationship between meanattackability and the technical attributes(3C's),

i. MeanAttackCompt = $Y + aCompt + \epsilon_1$ 4.1

    Where MeanAttackComp denotes the attackability due complexity(Comp) an "t" indicates the time element, that the expression is in time domain. Y indicate the point at which at which is expression was plot Y-X axis it could intercept the Y axis. While "a" in the expression represent the gradient of graph which is a limit of the rate of MeanAttackability per unit change in Complexity. ϵ_1 indicates the random error at time t = 0.

    The assumption for this metrics is there is positive correlation between Meanattackability and Complexity(Compt) . That the model is statistical model showing causal relationship. It satisfies Size(I) and Size(II) property as defined in section 2.6.2.

ii. MeanAttackCohent = $X + bCohent + \epsilon_2$ 4.2

    Where MeanAttackCohen is meanattackability due to cohesion(cohen), X is Y Axis intercept , b is gradient and ϵ_2. The Expression is in the time domain.

    The assumption for this metric is there is correlation between Meanattackability and Cohesion . It satisfies Size(I) and Size(II) property (section 2.6.2.) .

    However from literature it has been stated that the cohesion scale may not be linear. If this be the case regression analysis will be checked for quadratic function.

In that case : $\text{MeanattackCohen}_t = X + b_1 \text{cohen}_t + b_2 \text{cohen}^2 t + \epsilon_2$

Where b_1 and b_2 are coefficients of cohen and cohen^2 respectively

iii. $\text{MeanattackCoup}_t = Z + c\text{Coup}_t + \epsilon_3$ 4.3

It is time domain expression indicating a causal relationship between meanattackability due to coupling (coup). Where Z is intercept on Y axis, c is the gradient of the linear graph and ϵ_3 is the random error.

The assumption for this metrics is there is positive correlation between Meanattackability and Coupling . It satisfies Size(I) and Size(II) property . Metrics has been verified to be true by Liu& Traore.(2009). The other two are extension of this metric as applied to complexity and cohesion.

iv. $\text{TechMeanAttack} = (Y-X+Z) + (a\text{Compt} - b\text{Cohen}_t + c\text{Coup}_t) + (\epsilon_1 - \epsilon_2 + \epsilon_3)$ 4.4

Metric (iv) is a new metric defined as a summation of expressions (5.2,5.3 &5.4) of the three attributes working together. It is the Technical MeanAttackability(TechMeanAttack).It satisfies Size (I –III). Coupling and Cohesion work in opposition to each other hence the negative sign in the expression. If cohesion as a result of experiment it found that cohesion attackability relationship is a quadratic then expression (5.4) will change to

$\text{TechMeanAttack} = (Y-X+Z) + (a\text{Compt} - b_1\text{Cohen}_t - b_2\text{Cohen}^2 t + c\text{Coup}_t)$
$+ (\epsilon_1 - \epsilon_2 + \epsilon_3)$

v.   Predictive technical attackability metric

$= 1/3 \{(Y-X+Z) + (a\text{Comp}_t - b\text{Cohen}_t + c\text{Coup}_t) + (\epsilon_1 - \epsilon_2 + \epsilon_3)\}$ 4.5

The purpose of the metric is to try and predict the attackability of software systems knowing the three technical attributes. For this metric the 1/3 is due to probability arising from the sample space of three attributes. For the normalized case and taking discrete values for the attributes then metrics should give us a theoretical maximum of 1 and theoretical minimum of zero. This is within what is expected of probability, a maximum of 1 and minimum of 0.

4.4 Social Attackability Metrics

The metric is defined as a summation of each attributes probabilities as indicated in Figure 4b .Where a,b,c,d,e,f and h represents the probability measures for human traits (greed, TimePressure(Timep), Kindness(Kind), Dishonesty(Dish), Herd, Social compliance(socom) and Dist(Distraction).

(i)SocAttack =aGreed +bTimep +cKind+dDish+eHerd +fSocom +hDist   4.6

Social attackability (SocAttack) represents the system attack due to human traits/attributes that make one susceptible to social engineering attack.

The attributes are measured as percentile scale and taking the floor and ceiling function for attributes i.e. 0 and 1. Then theoretical maximum value is 7 since a, b, c, d, e, f and h have values between 0 and 1 and the attributes taking the discrete case have values varying from 0-1.. The minimum value for metrics will be zero.

(iii)   Predictive SocAttack metrics= 1/7(aGreed +bTimep +cKind+dDish+eHerd +fSocom +hDist).   4.7

Prediction will look at the possibility of even happening and seven attributes have equal probability of occurring hence 1/7. This multiplies equation 5.6. Since the theoretical maximum of equation 4.6 is   7 and minimum is 0. The theoretical maximum and minimum of equation 4.7 are 1 and 0 respectively. This falls within the range of probability and also satisfies Size (I-III).

4.5 Holistic attackability metrics

The metrics is defined as composite of technical and social.

Holistic attackbility metric={ TechAttack, SocAttack).   ={ $((Y-X+Z)+(aComp_t-bCohent +cCoupt) +(\epsilon_1- \epsilon_2+\epsilon_3))+(aGreed +bTimep +cKind+dDish+eHerd +fSocom +hDist,)$ 4.8

Predictive Holistic attackability metric = ½(TechAttack, SocAttack).   4.9

Since TechAttack and SocAttack has maximum value of 1 and minimum of 0.

Then the predictive holistic attackability metrics is also within range. From a theoretical aspect the metrics are theoretical validity for they are within Briand et al.(1998) size metrics evaluation criteria. They are also valid from the probability theory perspective. However empirical validation has to be done.

4.6 Attackability Metrics Algorithm

Once the metrics have be established their need to automate the collection of this metrics. The researcher discus an approach that could be used based on matrix multiplication. Consider the multiplication of row and column matrixes

A_{11} A_{12} and $\begin{matrix} B_{11} \\ B_{12} \end{matrix}$ The product $= A_{11}.B_{11} + A_{12}.B_{21}$.

The result is scalar value, a numeral. This concept can be adopted in an automated collection of the social and technical metrics. This we require that coefficient of attributes be read into row matrix and attributes into column matrix then follow the algorithms described below..

Consider the SocAttack metric

SocAttack =aGreed +bTimep +cKind+dDish+eHerd +fSocom +hDist.

The algorithm is:

(i)   Read in a, b, c, d, e, f , &h into row matrix

(ii)   Read in (Greed ,Timep, Kind, Dishon , Herd, Socomp,&Dist) into a column matrix

(iii)   Let A[k] = multiplying (i) &(ii)

(iv)   SocAttack = a[k]

(v)   Predictive SocAttack = (iv)*1/7

(vi)   End

Pseudo code

The coefficients in equation 5.6 that is a, b, c,d,e,f and h can be written into a row matrix and the attributes can written into a column matrix, where takes values of 1or 0.

A[i]=[a, b, c, d, e, f , h]

A[j] = [Greed ,Timep, Kind, Dishon , Herd, Socomp, Dist]$^{-1}$

For (A[j] = 0 A[j] < 8 A[j++])

A[k] =$\sum$ A[i].A[j]$^{-1}$

    A[i++]

    Next A[j]

SocAttack = A[k]

Predictive SocAttack = 1/7 A[k].

End

Considering TechAttack Metric

TechMeanAttack = $(Y-X+Z)+(aCompt-b_1Cohent-b_2Cohen^2t +cCoupt) +(\epsilon_1- \epsilon_2+\epsilon_3)$.

Considering case $Cohen^2t$ not ignored.

Algorithm is:

(i)   Read **$\epsilon1, \epsilon2, \epsilon3$**

(ii)   let e = **$\epsilon1- \epsilon2+\epsilon3$**

(iii)   read Y,X,Z

(iv)   Let W = Y-X+Z

(v)   Read a,b_1 & c into row matrix

(vi)   Read b_2 & Cohen

(vii) Let k= $b2*cohen^2$

(viii) Read complexity, cohesion & coupling into column matrix

(ix)   Let A[r] = (v)* (viii)

(x)   TechAttack = (vii)+(ii)+ (iv) +(ix)

(xi)   Predictive TechAttack=1/3(x)

(xii) End

    Pseudocode

Read a, b1,b2 ,c, y,x,z, $\epsilon_1, \epsilon_2, \epsilon_3,$ complexity, cohesion & coupling

A[m] = [a -b c]

A[n] = [complexity cohesion coupling]$^{-1}$

Where an attribute takes the value = 1 or 0

For (A[n] = 0 A[n] < 4 A[n++])

$A[r] = \sum A[m].A[n]^{-1}$

$A[m++]$

Next n

TechAttack $= (y+x+z)+ A[r] +(\epsilon_1+ \epsilon_2+ \epsilon_3)+ b_1*cohen^2$

Predictive TechAttack $= 1/3$(TechAttack)

End

Consider Holistic Attackability metric

(i)Holistic Attackability metric = [TechAttack SocAttack]

(ii) Predictive Holistic Attackability Metric = ½ (predict TechAttack + Predictive SocAttack)

Algorithm

A[h] = [TechAttack SocAttack]

A[p] =½ (predictive TechAttack + Predictive SocAttack)

End

4.5 Summary

In this chapter, six attackability metrics were defined and for each, it was indicated whether it is empirically sound. The six metrics were: predictive TechAttack, Predictive SocAttack , TechAttack, SocAttack . Predictive Holistic Attackability & Holistic Attackability. Algorithm and pseudo code to determine each have been given.

CHAPTER 5: EXPERIMENTAL METRICS VALIDATION RESULTS

5.1 Introduction

From theoretical validation of design metrics so designed appear to meet the threshold for size metrics. But for metrics to be useful in industrial context, they require empirical validation. The section discuss exploratory experiments that were initially done to test various concepts of the technical metrics and final Validation experiments that were carried out on twelve sample java application software's, most downloaded from sourceforge.org and other areas. Social metrics were derived from a questionnaire to sample population comprising of: lecturers, practicing technical staff and security staff at JKUAT and MMUST public Universities. Master students in Software engineering and Information Technology with experience in the area of security were also included.

5.2 Experimental preparation

Before conducting any experiments it important that preparation is done to ensure that the correct data is collected. The subjects are people sampled in social metrics data collection while the objects are various soft wares designed or downloaded for tests on technical aspect of internal attributes of software.

5.2.1 Subjects selection

The subjects were chosen mainly from the academic staff of Jomo Kenyatta University of Agriculture and Technology and Masinde Muliro University of science and technology. The criteria were at least a Master degree holder in Information technology or related field. However technical staffs who have registered for Master degree in the said Universities were considered on the basis that they have hands on experience.

5.2.2 Experimental materials

Materials required were three networked computers, one computer act as server, one a client and as an attack computer. Java software based application. The experiments were categorized as either exploratory or validation experiments. For the exploratory experiments, modules were selected or written such that exhibited one of the seven type's of cohesion while trying to maintain complexity constant. The other modules were written with varying McCabe's complexity factor while attempting to retain the other variables constant. For the validation experiment software were sourced from various sources and used in the experiments.

5.3Experimental planning

Experimental planning means going through whole process mentally and to determine requirements, sequence, resource required, time required and any challenges that may arise.

5.3.1 Experimental context –

The goal of the experiment was to determine the type of relationship between the chosen attributes and attackability and thereof consider the possibility of modeling the individual or/and the combined relationship, finally to validate the model.

5.3.2 Variables – IVs, and DVs.

Table 7(b) Independent & DependantVariables Source (Author)

Serial No	Independent Variable(IV)	Dependent variable	Type Measurement	Moderating Variables
	Complexity	Attackability	Quantitative	
	Cohesion	Attackability	Quantitative	
	Coupling	Attackability	Quantitative	
	Dishonesty	Attackability	Qualitative	
	Distraction	Attackability	Qualitative	
	Greed/need	Attackability	Qualitative	
	Kindness	Attackability	Qualitative	
	Time pressure	Attackability	Qualitative	
	Social compliance	Attackability	Qualitative	
	Herd mentality	Attackability	Qualitative	

Table 7(b) shows variables involved in the experiments. Type of measurement is quantitative is a lab exercise was carried out and actual measurement carried out. The qualitative measurements are based on 5 point Lickert scale questionnaire.

5.3.3 Hypotheses –

The null hypotheses to be tested using **SPSS** are listed in Table 8.

Table 8 Hypotheses Source (Author)

	Null Hypothesis
H_{o1}	The correlation between attackability and complexity is not significant
H_{o2}	The correlation between attackability and cohesion is not significant
H_{o3}	The correlation between measured mean attackability and calculated mean attackability for derived model is not significant

5.3.4 Experimental design –

In the exploratory experiments different objects were used and to test for attackability based on whether the cohesion or complexity was the independent variable. For the validation experiment all the three attributes were considered concurrently as the test was done. In survey the same questionnaire was answered by different subjects.

5.3.5 Threats to validity

Construct Validity. Values obtained for the first and second experiments are objective measurement hence can be considered to have construct validity. However the measurements for social metrics are subjective and are based on the perception of the subjects. However since these are experts in the area of security, the measurement can be considered valid.

Internal validity

In exploratory experiment since all objects were specifically constructed for the task at hand and hence focused to a specific task, the experiments were internally valid. However, the validation experiments were generalized and the issue of internal validity could arise. The subjects for the survey, could have differences among themselves like, experience, motivation fatigue among others could arise. The subjects were given at least two weeks to answer the questions, to allow them to answer them when they were most comfortable. The entire subjects were also picked from a University setting. It was then hoped that the internal validity would not be an issue.

External validity

The Exploratory Experiments could easily suffer from issues of externally validity since it could be argued that the environment was artificial. To overcome this validation experiment were performed on sample software reducing the effect of external validity. For the survey design apart from the questionnaire another validation tool was administered to the practicing security experts in non academic institutions the survey design could be considered to have external validity.

5.4Experimental operation

This section will describe how the experiments were operationalised. The section highlights the experimental process, the validation experiments setting and environment. Finally lists the experimental package required.

5.4.1 Experimental process

The Social metrics measurement were derived pilot survey using ten members of MMUST in the month of October 2012.Analysis of the data and modification of questionnaire was done in November and the results of the finding presented in a

PhD seminar held in November 2012. Request to conduct research within MMUST and JKUAT were made in November 2012.

Questionnaires issued in January 2013. Data collected was cleaned and inputted in SPSS as data was received. By April the 35 0f the 60 questionnaires issued had been returned. Out of the returned questionnaires four were found out range compared with the rest and were discarded.

Pilot experiment was done between the months of February and April 2013.The goal was to establish whether it were possible to come up with model. The experiment was exploratory. The study adopted an approach used in physical science where, when one is testing the relationship between various independent variables and single dependent variables you try to hold the others constant as far as possible. When testing for the relationship between attackability and cohesion, complexity was held constant. We set out to measure attackability as the software complexity increased but finding soft wares whose complexity increased gradually was an issue. So we wrote small soft wares with McCabe's complexity varying from 1 to five .The measurement of this metric was manually done using the fact that McCabe's Cyclomatic complexity factor $V(G)=$ Number of closed regions+ 1   5.1

The work load and corresponding time were measured. After establishing an optimum workload and time the workload was increased and the corresponding time measured with complexity been held constant.

Complexity was then varied, an optimum load and time established and the process of increasing the workload and monitoring the corresponding time repeated The above procedure was repeated for cohesion. Coupling and attackability had being modeled earlier and the researcher took the existing model and wished to test its validity in a different environmental testing.

The data collected was analyzed and formed the basis of a second PhD seminar presentation. However it was criticized for choice of the environment and lacking in external validity. It was suggested that validation experiments be done using open source soft wares and measured complexity, cohesion and coupling metrics

5.4.2 Validation Experiments

The experiments were conducted in April 2013 in MMUST laboratory. Software objects were download from SourceForge.net, planetary.org and some from MMUST development house. The software downloads were recompiled to ensure that they were running, and then a variable timing loop was introduced into the appropriate sections. The timer tool was based on nanotimer class which is part of the java.lang.* . For measuring complexity, coupling and cohesion a JHawk tool was used.

Three Laptops were connected using a wireless connection after the formation of a Test Home group. Figure 5 shows the wireless network that was used in carrying out the experiment s both at pilot stage and validation. The only difference being the soft wares being used and use a Jhawk tool to measure the internal attributes in the validation test.

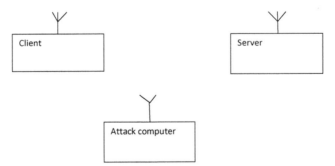

Figure 5 Test network (source Author)

The client requests for services from the server and the attack computer requested similar services but an increasing load, the aim being to flood the network.

100

5.4.3 Experimental package

Table 9 lists all materials that were used for experiment one and two.

Table 9 list of materials Source (Author)

S/No	Item	Description
1	Jhawk java metrics tool	Jhawk 5.1
2	Windows seven operating system	Microsoft
3	Java	JDk 1.6.1
4	Wamp/Xamp sever	database
5	3 Laptops	Two Mobile workstations Intel i5 and Dell Intel i3 all 2 duo core
4	University examination Card system	MMUST development house
5	Banksys	Planent.org
6	Airline booking systems	Planet.org
7	ATM	Sourceforge.net
8	Library management system	Sourgeforge.net
9	Payroll system	MMUST development house
10	Student information management sys	MMUST development house
11	Client server application	Source forge
12	Simple calculator	Source forge
13	Scientific calculator	Source forge
14	Maths application software	MMUST Development house
15	Validation application	MMUST development house
16	Database and interface test complexity as various modules are added(pilot Experiments	This was developed to provide an interface of attack for various modules to calling different modules to change complexity
12	Modules illustrate the various cohesions	Use in cohesion analysis -pilot

5.5 Data analysis and presentation

This section explains how data analysis was done and finding presented. The data highlighted is for complexity & cohesion testing for pilot experiments. Then data for validation experiment is also analyzed and presented. To illustrate how the process was carried out using the JHawk tool, a sample application the PayRoll is used and the corresponding screenshot displayed. Data analysis from the social metrics data gathering is also analyzed and presented.

5.5.1 Complexity testing.

Pilot experiment tests on complexity modules considered the fact that we were interested in service oriented architecture software; each module was considered a service to be called. Each was assumed to have the same complexity. Calling one module was considered equivalent to McCabes complexity of single region hence a complexity of one. Adding modules added complexity as shown in Table 10 plus the result of attacking the system. Meanattackability was determined by measurement of loads and time as required from the definition of attackabililty.

Table 10 Test Modules. Source (Author)

Module	Complexity	MeanAttackbility
Add	1	0.98
Add + Edit	2	1.04
Add + Edit+ Print	3	1.01
Add + Edit +Print+ Backup	4	1.14
Add+ Edit + Print + Backup + Delete	5	1.16

5.5.2 Cohesion testing

Modules were written to specifically test one of standard cohesion types as shown in the Table 11.Cohesion is normally measured on scale of 0 to 1 for the best and worst cohesion respectively.

102

Table11 Cohesion modules Source (Author)

Module	Cohesion	MeanAttackability
Coincidental	1.00	0.21
Logical	0.85	0.27
Temporal	0.68	0.32
Procedural	0.51	0.39
Communication	0.34	0.50
Sequential	0.17	0.40
Functional	0.00	0.32

5.5.3 Validation experimental data

Figure 6 illustrate the welcome screenshot of JHawk tool that was used to measure the complexity, cohesion, coupling metrics for the software application. A detailed explanation of the process of using the tool can be found in JHawk documentation manual an abridged version is given in appendix 4. The researcher uses the PayRoll application to illustrate the process that was used by showing screenshots taken in the process. To proceed from Figure 6, we select the "Analyze a set of java files to create new set of Java metrics data" button. This leads to Figure 7 screenshot. This allows one to selecting the files desired from a drive.

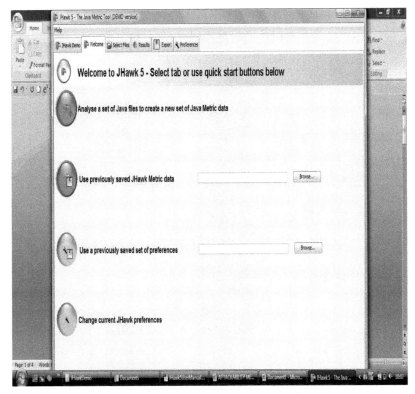

Figure 6 Jhawk Tool Welcome Screenshot Source(Author)

The screen is subdivided into left and right panel. On the left panel indicates that drive H has been selected and PayRoll application highlighted chosen. The Content of the Payroll application is shown on the lower section of left panel. Below the left panel are two buttons "Select All" and "Select File". By clicking on "Select All" all the Java files in the application will be pasted on the right panel as shown in Figure 7. To proceed we click on the analyze button. This leads us to Figure 8 screenshot

104

Figure 7 Select File Screen shot(Author)

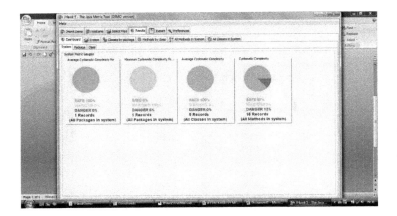

Figure 8 Dashboard Screenshot source (Author)

This displays a gauge for the complexity showing areas why there are classes whose complexity has exceed a set limit. The results tab button is highlighted so is Dashboard button. Along the Dashbutton are other buttons such as : System, Classes by package, methods by classes, All methods in the system and All classes in system. Using the PayRoll Java files selected we shall illustrate the results displayed by clicking each of the buttons.

To view the results at a system level we click on "System" button and Figure 9 is displayed.

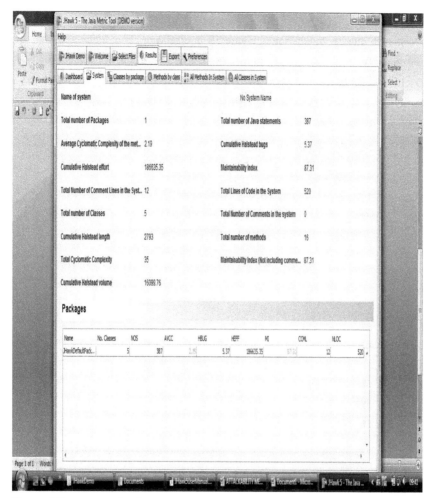

Figure 9 System results Screen shots

It shows the number of classes for a PayRoll application which is 5. Number of Java statements (NOS) 387 and Average Cyclomatic complexity of method as 2.19. Also displayed are: Total cyclomatic complexity 35, Total number of line codes, total number of the methods 15, and other Halstead measures.

Clicking on classes per packages Figure 10 is displayed. This figure lists the five classes and for each class, the No of methods per class, the lack of cohesion (LCOM) , AVCC and Response for Class(RFC) among others are indicated. The three metrics of interest are: LCOM cohesion metric, AVCC complexity metric and RFC a coupling metric.

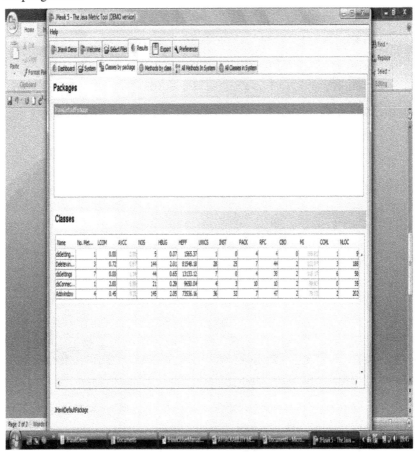

Figure 10 Classes results screenshot source (Author)

To view the result of analysis of each method the "Method by class button is selected leading to Figure 11. The classes appear on the upper part of right panel. From here one selects the class of interest.

In the displayed AddWindow class has been selected.

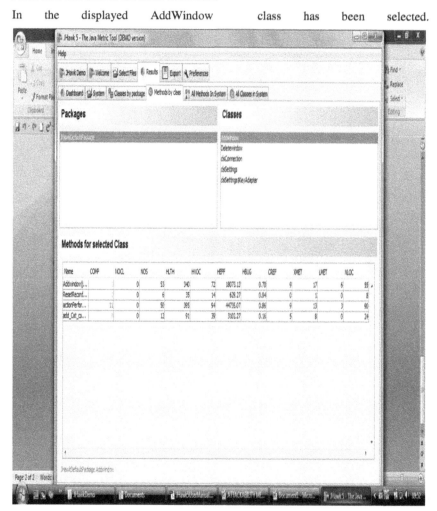

Figure 11 Methods Per class results Source(Author)

The data displayed in the complexity per method and on colored screen any complexity above ten will be shown in red color indicating that this method is too complexity and should be refactored. In Figure 11 ActionPerformed is the most complex with a complexity of 11 for the selected class. Selecting any other class will result with a metric analysis for that method being displayed

Clicking on " All Methods In System " button in displays Figure 12.

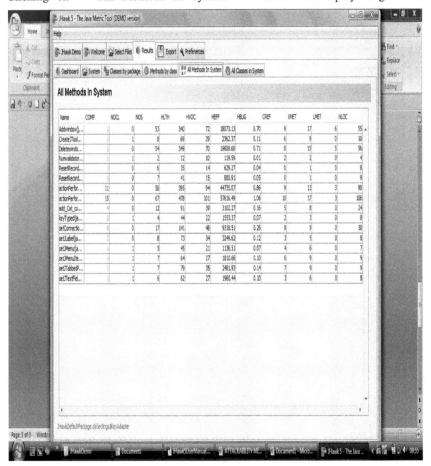

Figure 12 All Method in System Results Source(Author)

This displays the data analysis for all methods in the system.

Finally clicking on "classes in System" displays the result of the analysis and class level. Since the researcher interest were metric at the design level. The class metrics are appropriate. For the PayRoll system the results are displayed in Figure 13.

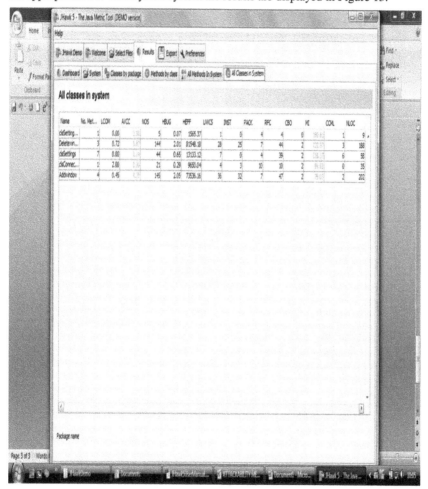

Figure 13 All Classes in System results source (Author)

Different software were analyzed using a Jhawk tool that analyses a software to various level, since the authors interest was at a class level, only the average class metrics were considered.

To illustrate the process of the Payroll application package was used and thereafter the results for the application software given. Table 12(a) shows the extracted metrics for readability and showing how the data in Table 12(b) was derived. The average metric for all classes and for each type was the metric used in the analysis.

Average class complexity = Total class complexity/(total no of classes) .   6.2

Table 12(b) shows the results of Average Metrics, Measured Meanattack is measured as a result

Table 12(a) PayRoll Metrics data

S/No	ClassName	LCOM	AVCC	RFC
1	clsSetting&keyadapter	0.00	2	4
2	delete Window	0.72	5.67	44
3	clsSetting	0.00	1.14	39
4	clsConnection	2.00	5	10
5	AddWindow	0.45	4.25	47
6	average metric value	0.63	3.61	28.80

of the experiment and CalMeanattack the expected output for Attackability as result measured metrics for independent variables being applied to the model.

Table 12(b) Metrics data Source (Author)

	Software application	Complexity AVCC	LCOM (Mean)	Coupling (mean)	Meanattack (measured)	CalMeanattack
1	ATM	3.33	.00	10.00	1.30	2.30
2	BankSys	3.22	.34	26.00	1.35	2.15
3	Simple Calculator	2.08	.00	12.00	.95	1.99
4	Scientific Calculator	7.08	.08	18	1.57	2.09
5	Payroll	3.61	0.63	28.80	0.94	1.90
6	Airline booking system	2.34	.04	16	1.1	2.09
7	Clientserver Application	2.33	.34	19.00	1.00	2.02
8	University Examination and Card system	3.00	.32	32.00	1.00	2.15
9	Student information management system	5.00	0.40	30.00	1.19	2.09
10	Mathematics application	1.00	0.6	15	0.86	1.83
11	Validation application	1.00	0.8	12	0.65	1.8
12	Library system	3.00	.40	23	1.00	1.96

The H_{03} was the Hypothesis of interest and there paired sample statistics were considered on the two MeanAttack. Table 13 standard deviation and standard mean error.

Table 13 **Paired Samples Statistics Source (Author)**

		Mean	N	Std. Deviation	Std. Error Mean
Pair 1	MEAN ATT	1.0758	12	.24545	.07085
	CALA TT	2.0225	12	.16074	.04640

5.5.4 Questionnaire data validation

Validity of a tool seeks to identify whether the tool will collect the required data. To validate this questions a pilot bookwas carried out on ten experts. To increase the reliability of tool the test –retest approach of the questionnaire development was adopted. Table 14 shows the results of the pilot study.

Table 14 Validating Questionnaire Tool source (Author)

Attributes/trait	Test	Retest	Deviation
Distraction	37	44	+7
Social Compliance	27	38	+11
Herd Mentality	32	34	+2
Dishonesty	50	39	-11
Kindness	41	38	-3
Time Pressure	38	44	+6
Greedy/need	48	38	-10

A deviation +2 (+26 +-24 =+2) is not significant and this was corrected by rephrasing questions that had issues. The tool could then be considered valid and reliable. A Cronbach alpha of greater than 0.7 is recommended for a tool be considered internally consistent, however if the number of comparisons are few the tool may give low values (Cronbach 1951).

5.5.5 Subjects Demographic data.

The Research set out to find out demographic information on the subjects taking part in survey, the results are shown in Tables 15 (a, &b)

Table 15a Gender Source (Author)

		Frequency	Percent	Valid Percent	Cumulative Percent
Valid	MALE	25	80.6	80.6	80.6
	FEMALE	6	19.4	16.1	96.8
					100.0
	Total	31	100.0	100.0	

The table indicates that 80.6% of the subjects were male while 19.4% were female. This generally reflects the state of affairs in the field of interest.

Table 15b: AGE Source(Author)

		Frequency	Percent	Valid Percent	Cumulative Percent
Valid	BTW 20-30 YRS	12	38.7	38.7	38.7
	BTW 30-40 YRS	10	32.3	32.3	71.0
	BTW 40-50 YRS	7	22.6	22.6	93.5
	ABOVE 50 YRS	2	6.5	6.5	100.0
	Total	31	100.0	100.0	

115

5.5.6 Technical metric Results

This section describes the correlation results, displays scatter diagrams and tables with correlation coefficient (Pearson, or Tau-b) for complexity vs. attackability, coupling vs. attackability, and Meanattackability vs. calattackability.

5.5.6.1 Correlations

Table 16: Kendall's Tau-b Correlation Results for Complexity Metrics and Attackability

Metric	Coefficients	p-value(1-tailed)
COMP	0.800*	0.025

*=95% confidence

The results from Table 16, show that there is significant correlation between complexity and attackability and therefore the null hypothesis (H_{o1}) fails. The converse is true that such a correlation exists and is significant at 95% level of confidence. Figure14 shows the scatter plot of complexity and attackability.

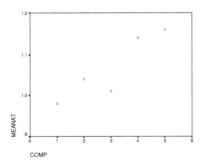

Figure 14 Scatter diagram for Complexity versus meanattackability Source(Author)

116

Table 17 shows the results of correlation between cohesion and attackability and the correlation is significant at 95% level of confidence. The null hypothesis H_{02} stating that such a correlation is not significant fails and the converse is true.

Table 17: Kendall's Tau-b Correlation Results for Cohesion Metric and Attackability

Metric	Coefficients	p-value(1-tailed)
COHEN	0.619*	0.025

*=95% confidence

The Scatter plot is shown in Figure 15

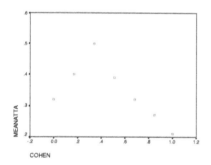

COHEN

Figure 15 Scatter diagram of attackability and cohesion Source (Author)

Table 18 shows the results of correlation between experimentally measured meanattackability and calculated meanattackability by applying the 3C'S metrics into the model. The null hypothesis H_{03} stating that it is not significant fails and the converse holds. It shows that it is significant at 0.01 levels. While Table 19 shows the T tests for paired samples.

117

Table 18 Pearson correlation between Calculated and Measured attackability

		CALATT	MEANATT
CALATT	Pearson Correlation	1	.771(**)
	Sig. (1-tailed)	.	.002
	N	12	12
MEANATT	Pearson Correlation	.771(**)	1
	Sig. (1-tailed)	.002	.
	N	12	12

** Correlation is significant at the 0.01 level (1-tailed).

Table 19 Paired Samples Correlations Source (Author)

		N	Correlation	Sig.
Pair 1	MEANATT & CALATT	12	.771	.003

Table 20 shows the T tests on paired difference and suggest that difference is not significant

Table 20 Paired differences Source (Author)

		Paired Differences					t	df	Sig. (2-tailed)
		Mea n	Std. Deviati on	Std. Error Mean	95% Confidence Interval of the Difference				
					Low er	Uppe r			
Pair 1	MEAN ATT - CALA TT	-.946 7	.15882	.04585	-1.04 76	-.8458	-20.6 48	11	.000

5.5.6 .2 Regression

This section gives a description of regression results followed by necessary diagrams &tables for various hypotheses.

Complexity versus Attackability

The results indicate the R Squared term is 0.829 meaning that knowing a complexity will can predict Mean attackability 83% of the times. It also suggest a linear relation with b0 value of 0.9280 that is place where the corresponding curve cuts the Y axis and b1 of 0.0460 which is the gradient of the curve that is dy/dx

Table 21 Regression of Complexity versus Attackability.

Independent: COMP

Dependent	Rsqd.	f.	F	Sigf	b0	b1
MEANAT	LIN	.829	3	14.56	.032	.9280

MEANAT LIN .829   3   14.56 .032 .9280 .0460

Figure 16 shows the corresponding graph

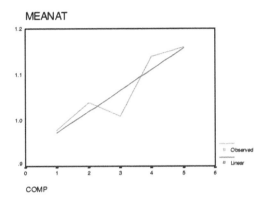

Figure 16 Graph of Complexity versus Atackability   Source Author

Table 22 shows the result of the regression between Cohesion and Attackability. The table shows the results of taking the curve to be linear and quadratic. If liner R^2 is 0.388 meaning that knowing cohesion we could predict the attackability 40% of the time which would be poor prediction. While assuming the relationship to be quadratic R^2 is 0.82 meaning that we could predict attackability 82 % percent of the time. Any prediction over 70 % is considered appropriate. Hence the appropriate model is quadratic with b0=0.3434 , b1=0.4412 the coefficient of Cohen and b2 = -0.6020 the coefficient of cohen^2

Table 22 Regression of Cohesion versus Attackability
Independent: COHEN

Dependent	Mth	Rsq	d.f.	F	Sigf	b0	b1	b2
MEANATTA	LIN	.388	5	3.17	.135	.4272	-.1631	
MEANATTA	QUA	.820	4	9.11	.032	.3434	.4412	-.6020

Figure 18 shows cohesion attackability graph

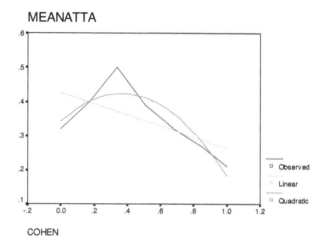

Figure 17 the Cohesion versus attackability curve Source (Author)

Figure 18 show a regression graph of the measured attackability versus calculated attackability. A linear relationship suggest that the model predict the measured value

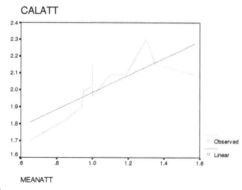

within an error margin,

Figure 18 Regression graph between the measure attackability and the calculated attackability

5.5.7 Social Metric results

This section presents and analysis the results of the social metrics. Table 23 shows the result of measure of the each of seven personality traits as measure of its contribution to social attackability

Table 23 Social metrics measure for Personality traits Source (Author)

Attribute/trait	Test	Retest	Mean
Dish	0.884	0.819	0.85
Dist	0.6451	0.819	0.73
Socomp	0.839	0.826	0.83
Herd	0.748	0.8	0.77
Kind	0.703	0.78	0.76
Timep	0.729	0.806	0.77
Greed	0.832	0.69	0.76

The table 23 shows the result of test retest and the metric is the computer as mean. Each was derived as of descriptive analysis on SPSS software. The values were derived based on weighting of questionnaire that used {5,4,3,2,1} as weights to the content of 5 scale Lickert scale that Strongly agree, agree, do not know(DNK), disagree and strongly disagree.

Table 23(a) Dishonest –Test Source (Author)

DISH

		Frequency	Percent	Valid Percent	Cumulative Percent
Valid	DISAGREE	2	6.5	6.5	6.5
	DNK	2	6.5	6.5	12.9
	AGREE	8	25.8	25.8	38.7
	STRONGLY AGREE	19	61.3	61.3	100.0
	Total	31	100.0	100.0	

Count of outcome for DISH j= (5*(no of strongly agree)+4*(no of agree) +3*(no of DNK) + 2*(no of disagree) +1*(Strongly disagree)   6.3

DISH=95+32+6+4=137

From equation 4.6 then P(DISH)= 137/155=0.884

Table 23(b) Dishonest –Retest Source(Author)

DISH1

		Frequency	Percent	Valid Percent	Cumulative Percent
Valid	DNK	6	19.4	19.4	19.4
	AGREE	16	51.6	51.6	71.0
	STRONGLY AGREE	9	29.0	29.0	100.0
	Total	31	100.0	100.0	

Count of outcome for DISH1 j= (5*(no of strongly agree)+4*(no of agree) +3*(no of DNK) + 2*(no of disagree) +1*(Strongly disagree)

DISH=45+64+18+ =127

From equation 4.6 then P(DISH1)= 127/155= 0.819
Mean Value P(DISH)= (0.884+0.816)/2 =0.85
This was entered in mean column in Table 23.
The values for other attributes were similarly determined.

5.5.8 Social Metrics Validation results

After getting the result of social metric the author tend validate the result by requesting five practicing security experts rate in scale of 1 to 10 to which given trait affects social attackability of a system. Table 24a shows the organization and job title of security expert used in validation. The data from this group was entered into an Excel spreadsheet for each of the attribute and mean determined referred as ValMean. This mean was converted into a value between 0 and 1. These means were also entered into an Excel worksheet together with mean result from sample population (sampleMean).

Table 24(a) Social metrics Validation Experts Company and job title

S/N0	Company	Job Title
1	Ministry of Finance - Treasury	Risk Analyst
2	Safaricom,	IT Security manager
3	Price Water house coopers	Security Analyst
4	Techmax Solutions Limited	Network security Engineer
5	Techmax Solutions Limited	Security Accounts Manager

The deviation between ValMean and Sample Mean was determined for each with ValMean used as reference. A mean deviation was determined and used to generate a corrected mean from sampleMean. Table 24(b)

Table 24b   Social Metrics Validation results and Correction of Metrics

Attribute	SampleMean	ValMean	Deviation	Corrected mean
Dish	0.85	0.64	-0.21	0.751
Dist	0.73	0.64	-0.09	0.631
Socomp	0.83	0.3	-0.53	0.731
Herd	0.77	0.94	0.17	0.671
kind	0.76	0.9	0.14	0.661
Timep	0.77	0.56	-0.21	0.671
Greed	0.76	0.8	0.04	0.661
MeanDeviation			-0.098571429	

5.6   Discussion

The section provides a discussion of the finding in the above sections. The discussion is based on the implication correlation and regression results of attackability versus complexity and attackability versus cohesion. Coupling versus attackability had be modeled earlier on and what this researcher was to assume it valid and test via hypothesis three whether this case. The implication of social metrics results is also highlighted.

5.6.1 Implications of correlation results for complexity vs. attackability,

This result indicates that complexity can be used to predict Meanttackability with 95% level of confidence. Regression analysis was performed and R squared value was .829 indicating that we can predict meanattackability knowing complexity 83% of the time. Hence a linear model is appropriate and is describe by:

Meanattackability= 0.928+0.046COMP   5.4

5.6.2 Implication results of Cohesion versus attackability results

For Kendall's tau_b correlation is significant at 0.05 because the p value = .025 which is less than 0.05 with a correlation coefficients of 0.619. We may then conclude cohesion may be used to predict attackability. However regression analysis was carried out assuming a linear model and assuming a quadratic model. The regression analysis for linear model showed Rsquared value of 0.388 meaning that knowing Cohesion we can predict attackability 38.8% of times. This is low and not an appropriate model. The R squared value quadratic model was 0.822 meaning that we can predict attackability 82.2% of the times knowing cohesion and this was considered good model and was adopted. The model is described by:

MeanattackCohen = 0.034 + 0.44COHEN -.06COHEN^2 5.5

5 .6.3 Implication of Coupling and attackability results

The bookassumed that model is valid for different environments other the Medical application it was initially tested on and set out test this relationship indirectly via hypothesis three. The result of testing H_{03} shows that the relation holds as assumed in the model. This implies that relationship is valid for the 12 softwares tested.

5.6.4 Implication of Measured Meanattackbility Vs Calculated MeanAttackability

It had be assumed that modeling technical metric can be generated by taking the 3C's working together such that the technical attackability metric can be defined as:

Techattackability = (MeanattackComp + MeanattackCoup - MeanattackCohen). A negative sign to take care of the fact that coupling and cohesion appear to work in opposition. 5.6

$$=([0.928+0.046COMP]+[1.67+0.4COUP] -[0.34 + 0.44COHEN -.06COHEN^2])$$

Maximum value = 0.928+0.046+1.67+0.4 -0.34-0.44+0.06=2.324   5.7

Minimum value = 0   5.8

This equation was used experiment two where the 3C's measured for software and the meanattackability measured as well as calculated attackability (calAtt) determined. The correlation coefficient 0.77 indicates the equation can be used to predict the technical metric. Hence the metric though with error is valid since the error is not significant. The predictive technical attackability metric is then 1/3(Meanattackability Metrics)

The error in the results could be an indicator of other attributes not considered, or the attributes interacting with each other in more complex way. Another issue worthy of considerations is processor affinity which tended to affect the accuracy of the measurement.

5.6.5 The implication of the result on social metrics

This implies that the social attackability can be realized as

SocAttack =aGreed +bTimep +cKind+dDISH+eHERD +fSOCOMP +hDIST

=0.751DISH+0.661GREED+0.661KIND+ 0.671TIMEP + 0.631DIST + 0.671HERD + 0.731SOCOMP,   5.9

Max=0.751+0.661+0.661+0.671+0.631+0.671+0.731=4.777   5.10

$$\text{Min} = 0 \qquad\qquad\qquad 5.11$$

This implies could generate a metric within a range 4.777 and 0. The high value indicates the need for further social engineering training or awareness otherwise the people can is suffer from social engineering attack..

For a predictive metric we assume that each of the traits is equally likely with a probability of 1/7

Predictive Soattack =1/7(0.751DISH+ 0.661GREED+ 0.661KIND +0.671TIMEP +0.631DIST +0.671HERD+0.731SOCOMP)   5.12

Predictive SocAttack Max = 4.777/7 =0.682   5.13

Predictive SocAttack Min = 0/7 =0.0   5.14

This falls within the range of expected probability of between 0 and 1. The metrics is therefore valid and implies it can be used in predicting the social attackability of the operator in software system implying attackability of the system.

5.6.6 The implication of the Holistic metrics Results

Mathematical induction allows us to infer the correctness of some postulation starting with a valid case. In our case both TechAttack and SocAttack are valid on their own rights. Hence extending them to set and calling that set a holistic attackability metrics means the corresponding metrics is both correct and valid. Hence Holistic attackability Metrics =(TechAttack , SocAttack).   5.15

Substituting the values for Techattack & SocAttack

Holistic attackability Metrics ={([0.928+0.046COMP]+[1.67+0.4COUP] −[0.0390 + 0.1576COHEN   −.0162COHEN^2]), 0.751DISH+ 0.661GREED+0.661KIND +0.671TIMEP+0.631DIST+0.671HERD+0.731SOCOMP)}   5.16

Substituting the ceiling values for all the attributes results in

Holistic attackability Metric Max =(0.96 , 0.682)   5.17

Substituting the floor values for all the attributes results in

Holistic attackability Metric Min =(0 , 0).   5.18

The metrics holds and therefore can be used for holistic metrics. Holistic in that, it has Technical aspect and social aspect. Hence the system designers have a metric that will allow them, not only predict whether software system would successfully attacked due to the technical and attributes. He can then take the necessary mitigation measures.

Predictive Holistic attackability Metric = { Predictive TechAttack, Predictive ,

SocAttack)   5.19

Hence Predictive Holistic attackability Metric Max =1/2(0.96 , 0.682)   5.20

= 0.821 compared with and ideal of 1   5.21

Predictive Holistic Metric Min = ½(0, 0) = 0   5.22

The metrics fall within expected range of 1 and 0. It implies that they are valid and can be used for predicting holistically the attackability of software system.

5.7 Summary

This chapter has highlighted the experiments that were carried out, tests that were done and their results. The process of validation of metrics and finally concluded that the metrics the metrics are empirically sound. The metrics have been extended to include the predictive aspect. Finally the social and technical metrics have been combined to form the holistic predictive metrics. The results are within expected range and hence valid and can be used for evaluation of software systems.

CHAPTER SIX: CONCLUSION AND RECOMMENDATION

The book set out to provide a model of attackability measurement that could be used at architectural design level, to predict the ability of a software system to withstand denial of service attacks and social attacks. This was to be achieved through a series of specific objectives, research questions and three hypotheses. On whether this was achieved can be decided by establishing whether the specific objectives were met and the results of hypotheses testing.

The first specific objective the book set out to achieve was to find out what attributes affect attackability and postulate the type of relationship between the attackability and the attribute. From literature review ten attributes were established and classified into technical and social. Among the technical attributes identified were complexity, cohesion and Coupling. The relationship between coupling and attackability had been established earlier on. The book wished to test this on other soft wares and confirm if it holds. This was indirectly confirmed from third hypothesis in the testing. For complexity researchers had previously shown a positive correlation between attackability and the complexity but no modeling was done. The author took this relationship and tested it in hypothesis one. It was proved to be true and it was then modeled.

On Cohesion, from literature review it was established that there a relationship exists but it was considered to work in opposition to the relationship between coupling and attackability. Also the relationship between the worst cohesion and the best cohesion was considered not linear. This was tested and found to be the case in hypothesis two.

From literature review seven human traits/attribute were distilled it was assumed that each affected social attackability positively. No researcher had previously attempted to model any of the relationship. It was found that each is measured a percentile scale. But for the purpose of this research only the floor and ceiling functions were considered that is 0 and 1. The book concludes that objective one was successively achieved.

The second objective was to develop a holistic predictive attackability metrics model. It was holistic in that it combined social and technical aspects. The social aspect was to take care of attributes that make human beings susceptible to social engineering attacks while the technical part was to take care of internal software attributes that affect software attackability.

Social part was modeled as a probability model with the attributes forming a disjoint set. For each trait its contribution to attackability was measured using a Five point Licket and results weighted in scale of 5 to 1. This was later normalized to generate a probability whose value was between 1 and 0. The overall results were considered a union. This formed the social attackability model. To convert it into a predictive model a sample space of the seven attributes was considered introducing probability of 1/7.

Technical part was modeled as statistical model for each of the attributes. The three being statistical models were combined to form the technical attackability model. No researcher had attempted to do this before. The predictive aspect was derived by assuming that the sample space involved the three and hence each had probability of 1/3 and by introducing this model could be used as predictive model

To covert this into a holistic model the two models were combined. The three blocks then constituted the holistic attackability metric model whose output was considered to be {Techattack metric, and Socialattack metric}. Since the sample consists of only the two then introducing a probability ½ makes the model predictive. The holistic predictive attackability model has been developed and tested. The objective two was achieved.

The third objective was to generate attackability metrics from the model. This involved modeling each attribute and establishing a relation between the attribute and attackability. This was done for nine attributes. The relationship between attackability and coupling had been previous done and was assumed. It was combined with the other technical models to generate the technical attackability metrics model. The model and the corresponding metrics were experimental validated. This meant that coupling metrics was indirectly validated. The predictive metrics was also defined. This was the first attempt that authors are aware of modeling the 3C's together versus attackability.

Social metrics were combined to form a social attackability model and corresponding metrics. This was also the first attempt at modeling such a relationship and gives an objective tool to the managers in deciding when social engineering training may be required. The third objective was achieved.

The fourth objective was to validate the attackability metrics. This was done via experiment for the technical metrics through hypothesis three. The social metrics were validated via questionnaire that was issued to practicing system security professional. It can then be concluded that the objective four was realized. The authors went further to write down an algorithm that can be used in automating the metrics.

In conclusion six metrics were defined and validated. Relationship between the nine attributes and attackability was done. The coupling relationship was tested and confirmed to be true in a different test environment. The Technical attackability model combining the 3C's as well as Social attackability model was developed. Finally a holistic predictive attackability model was synthesized from the two.

A system with high attackability measure indicates a system that can be easily attacked. The system designer and project managers should aim for low values. The model has been published in the international journal of information communication technology research(Mbuguah et al. 2012). The journal also publication papers on social metrics derived from this research as well as another paper on experimental validation of the technical attackability metrics model(Mbuguah et al.2013) The Journal of emerging trends in computing and information Science published a paper on the algorithm as defined in this book(Mbuguah etal.2014) The authors then concludes all specific objectives well as general objective were satisfied. The model and metrics can be used as predictor of software systems attackability.

However, there were challenges that were encountered that may require further research that may lead to fine tuning the model and the corresponding metrics. It was found that processor affinity tended to affect the accuracy of the reading. Processor affinity is a tendency of a processor to have related instructions and loads them in its locality. In multiprocessor system, this means a given processor is assigned tasks and by prefetching instructions before a request speeding up the processing. There is need to carry out further research to see how this affects the accuracy of the results and introduce counter measures to overcome this problem or take care of it. For this research, this aspect was controlled by breaking up the load request pattern when readings indicated that the processor affinity is becoming an issue.

Further research should be carried out to determine how other attributes that could affect attackability. For instance it would be interesting to find out how the presence of a security mechanism affects the model. The other attributes should then be factored into the model and the metrics further refined. The tests were done on 12 java applications only; it would be interesting to find out whether Language of use has any effects. The book should be extended to large scale projects to see whether the models and metrics hold.

A tool like JHawk could be extended to measure the attackability of software as well. For the social engineering aspect, a tool could be developed that automates the procedure of gathering the data. A person may be asked a set of questions which could act as a measure of the stated attributes. This could then be incorporated into the algorithm for measuring the social attack ability metrics. The tool can be integrated with Jhawk Tool or any other tool that is capable measuring the software technical attributes to generate the overall holistic attackability of the system. It was also assumed that gender and age are not factors as far as social engineering is concerned. It would be interesting to investigate this aspect in future research and find out whether any affects the social attackability.

The software systems were tested for only denial of service attack. Further research should be carried out with other types of attacks to establish whether the model and metrics hold.

REFERENCE

Al, L. e. (2009). *The Psychology of Scams:Provoking and Commiting Errors Of , Judgement.* London: University of Exeter School of Psychology.

Alhazmi O. H. Y. K. (2007,). "Measuring, Analyzing and Predicting Security , Vulnerabilities , in Software Systems,". *Computers & Security, vol. 26, no. , 3*, pp. 219-228.

Allen, M. 2004. Social Engineering: A means to violate a computer system from , http://securitytechnet.com/resource/security/hacking/1365.pdf.

Alves-Foss J. and Barbosa S. (1995). Assessing Computer Security Vulnerability,. , *ACM , SIGOPS , Operating Systems Review 29,3 p. 3-13.* ACM.

Allsopp W. *Unauthorised Access: Physical Penetration Testing For IT Security , Teams*, chapter Planningyour physical penetration test, pages 11–28. Wiley, , 2009.

Andrews J. A. (2005.). *"How to Break Web Software",.* Addison-Wesley,

Atallah, M. J., Raskin, V., Hempelmann, C. F., Karahan, M.,Sion, R., Topkara, U., , and Triezenberg, K. E. 2002. Natural language Watermarking and , Tamperproofing. In F. A. P.Petitcolas, Ed. *Information Hiding: 5th , International Workshop, IH 2002, Proceedings.* Berlin: Springer, 196-210.

Baumrind D. Research using intentional deception. Ethical issues revisited. *The , American psychologist,*40(2):165–174, 1985.

Barrett N. Penetration testing and social engineering hacking the weakest link. , *Information Security Technical Report*, 8(4):56–64, 2003.

Beattie S, S. A. (2002). Timing the Application of Security Patches for Optimal , Uptime, *Proceedings of LISA: Systems Administration Conference.*

Bieman, J. M. and Ott, L. M., "Measuring Functional Cohesion," *IEEE Transactions on Software Engineering*, Vol. 20, No. 8, 1994, pp644-657.

Bishop, M., and Gates, C. 2008. Defining the Insider Threat. In *Proceedings of the , Cyber Security and Information Intelligence Research Workshop,* Paper #15.

Brackney, R., and Anderson, R. 2004. Understanding theinsider threat. In: *Proceedings of a March 2004 Workshop.*Technical report, RAND Corporation, Santa Monica, CA.

Briand, L.C., Morasca, S. and Basilli, V.R. 1996. Property-based software engineering measurement, *IEEE Transactions on Software Engineering* 22: 68-86.

Browne H.K, Arbaugh W.A, McHugh J, Fithen W.L, (2001). A Trend Analysis of. , *Exploitations, Proceedings of IEEE , Symposium on Security and Privacy. ,* IEEE.

Brocklehurst S, B. L. (,1994.). "On Measurement of Operational Security",. , *Proceedings of ,the 9th Annual Conference on Computer Assurance.*

Booch G.(2008) Measuring Architectural Complexity I E E E S o f t wa r e *P u b l i s h e d b y t h e I E E E C omp u t e r S o c i e t y*

Boyle G.J., Matthews G., and. Saklofske D.H (Eds.), *Handbook of personality , theory and testing: Vol. 2: Personality measurement and assessment.* London: Sage.

Buechler S.(2007) Statistical model in R *Department of mathematics 276b , hurley Hall*

Cattell, H.E.P, and Mead, A.D. (2007). The 16 Personality Factor Questionnaire , (16PF). Accessed on 31/12/http://www.psycometric .com/personality tests , 30/12/12

CERT. (2009). *Advisories.* US-CERT Vulnerabilities notes ,httt/www.org/advisories

CERT. (2009). National Cyber Alert System: Cyber Security Tip ST04-0141, from . http://www.us-cert.gov/cas/tips/ST04-014.html.

135

Chen J.(2004)   Effects of test anxiety, time pressure, ability and gender on ,
response aberrance. PhD dissertation, Ohio State University

Chou, J. Y. (2001). An Empirical Bookof Operating System Errors,. *Proceedings of
ACM ,Symposium on Operating System Design and Implementation* . ACM.

Chidamber *S.R.*, Kemere*r* C.F,(1994). "A Metrics Suite for Object Oriented ,
Design,". *IEEE Trans.,*   on *,Software Eng., vol. 20, no. 6,* , pp. 476-493.

Chowdhury   I.   and   Zulkermine M.   (2010,).   Can Complexity, Coupling, and ,
Cohesion Metrics be Used as , Early Indicators of Vulnerabilities? *SAC'10,* .
Sierre, Switzerland.: ACM.

Cialdini R.(2009) The Psychology of Influence, HarperCollins e-books

Code of Federal Regulations. Title 45: Public welfare department of health and ,
human services. part 46: Protectionof human subjects. pages 1–12. 2005.

Cornish D. B(1994). The procedural analysis of offending and its relevance for ,
situational , prevention. In R. V. Clarke, editor, *Crime Prevention Studies*,
volume 3,pages 151– 196.

Cornish D.B. & Clarke R.V.(2003). Opportunities, precipitators and criminal ,
decisions: A reply to Wortley's critique of situational crime prevention. ,
Crime Prevention Studies, 16:41–96,

Collins, M., Schweitzer, D. & Massey, D. 2008. CANVAS: a Regional Assessment ,
Exercise for Teaching Security Concepts. In *Proceedings of*
,   *the 12th Colloquium for Information Systems Security Education*, Dallas TX
Costa P.T. and McCrae R(2005) ,Trait theories of personality . Advanced personality
,   New York Plenum press
Cronbach, L. J. (1951). Coefficient alpha and the internal structure of tests. ,
*Psychometrika, ,   16,*297-334.

Dacier M. and Deswarte Y. (1994). Privilege Graph: An extension to the Typed , Access ,Matrix Model,. *Proceedings of European Symposium on Research in Computer ,Security*

Devedzic, V. 2002. Understanding Ontological Engineering. In *Communications of , the ACM*.

Dimkov T, Pieters W, &Hartel P(2010) Two methodologies for physical , penetration testing using social engineering,Distributed and Embedded , Security GroupUniversity of Twente, The Netherlands Copyright 2010 ACM

Distefano J.J.,Stubberud & Williams(1987) Feedback and Control Systems McGraw-Hill

Dolan, A. 2004. Social engineering. SANS Reading Room. Retrieved November , 2011from http://securitytechnet.com/resource/security/hacking/1365.pdf.

Favre C. G. (2009). *Security models.* P.Lafourcade.

Farahmand, F., and Spafford, E. H. 2010. Understanding Insiders: An Analysis of , Risk-Taking Behavior. *Information Systems Frontiers*.

Fenton E.N, Neil M. (1999.). A Critique of Software Defect Prediction Models, *IEEE Transaction on Software Engineering, VOL, 25, No. 3,* .

Fenton N. E.and Pfleeger S. L. (1997). *Software Metrics: A Rigorous andPractical , Approach,* . Boston, MA, USA,: PWS Publishing Co.

Fenton. N(1994) Software measurement: a necessary scientific basis. IEEE Trans. Software Engineering pp 199-206

Finn P. *Research Ethics: Cases and Materials*, The ethics of deception in , research, pages 87–118.Indiana University Press, 1995.

Finn P &Jakobsson M. Designing ethical phishing experiments. *Technology and , Society Magazine, IEEE*,26(1):46–58, Spring 2007.

Fridman-Noy, N., and Hafner, C. D. 1997. The State of the Art in Ontology Design: , A Survey and Comparative Review. *AI Magazine* 18(3): 53-74.

Goodman. Snowball sampling. *The Annals of Mathematical Statistics*, 32(1):148–, 170, 1961.

Gosling, S. D.; Rentfrow, P. J.; Swann Jr, W. B. (2003). "A very brief measure of the Big-Five personality domains". *Journal of Research in Personality*

Grice, H. P. 1975 Logic and conversation. In: P. Cole and J. L. Morgan, Eds. *Syntax, and Semantics. Vol.3. Speech Acts*. NewYork: Academic Press, 41-58

Guarino, N. 2004. Toward a Formal Evaluation of OntologyQuality. *IEEE intelligent , Systems* 19(4): 78-79.

Greenlees C. An intruder's tale-[it security]. *Engineering & Technology*, 4(13):55–, 57, 2009.

Harris, S. G. (2010). Emerging Markets:The coming African Tsunami of Information Insecurity. *Communicationms ACM* , 24-27.

msdn.microsoft.com/library/default.asp?url=/library/en-us/dncode/html/

Herzog P. OSSTMM   (2006)2.2–Open Source Security Testing Methodology , Manual,*Open source document, www.isecom.org/osstmm*,

Howard, J. P. (2003). Measuring Relative Attack Surfaces, . *Proceeding of , Workshop on , Advanced Developments in Software and System Security* .

Howard, M. (2003). ,*Fending Off Future Attacks by Reducing Attack Surface*,

http/www.safaricom.com

Islam S and Dong W.(2008) Human factors in software security risk management, , *LSMA'08 Leipzig, German ACM*

Janes, M. S. (2006,). "Identification of Defect-prone Classes in Telecommunication , Software Systems Using Design Metrics,. *" The Journal of Systems , &Software, vol. 176,* , pp. 3711-3734.

JHawk5 (2010) Documentation Standalone Manual *Virtual Machinery 1.0Content*

Kaur K, K. Minhas. (2009). Static and Dynamic Complexity Analysis of. World , Academy of Science, Engineering and

Keinan G.Friendland N, & Ben-Parath Y.(1987). Decision making under stress: Scanning of Alternatives under physical threat. *Acta Psychological, 64 219-228*

Kemerer, S. C. (1994,). "A Metrics Suite for Object Oriented Design,". *IEEE Trans. , on Software Eng., vol. 20, no. 6,* , pp. 476-493.

Kibeom L., Michael C., Ashton, David L., Morrison, John Cordery and Dunlop(2008) . HEXACO Model within Industrial organization environment. *Journal Occupational and Organizational Psychology 147-167*

Kvedar D., Nettis M & Fulton S.P(2010). The Use of formal Engineering techniques to identity weaknesses during computer Vulnerability competition . *United, States Air force Academy*

Lakhotia A,(1993) Ruled Based approach to computing module cohesion. 15th , *International conference on Software Engineering*

Lenat D.B(1990). Toward programs with common sense. Communication of the , ACM 33(8):30-49

Long j., Wiles J., Pinzon S.,and Mitnik K.D.(2008) No Tech Hacking: A Guide to , social Engineering, Dumpster Diving and Shoulder Surfing. Rockland MA: Syngress

Leverton J(2003) The Bubble Mania . *The part place Economist Volume X*

Levinson S.C(1983).Pragmatics.*Cambridge University Press*

Liu M . Traore I. (2004.). UML-based Security Measures of Software Products. *4th , International Conference on Application International of Concurrency to System Design (ACSD-04),.* Hamilton,Ontario, Canada, : ACSD-04).

Liu M.Y., Traore I. (2005). *Measurement Framework for Software Privilege based on User Interaction Analysis.* Victoria BC V8W 3P6, Canada: , University of Victoria, .

Liu M. Y. and Traore I.(2009). "Empirical Relations Between Attackabilityand , Coupling: A case study on DoS,". *in ACM proc. SIGPLAN Workshop on , Programming Languages and Analysis for security* (pp. pp. 57-64.). Ottawa Canada: ACM.

139

Liu M. Y. and Traore I.((2007). Complexity Measures for Secure Service-Oriented Architectures. *Third International Workshop on Predictor Models in Software Engineering (PROMISE'07)*. IEEE-COMPUTER SOCIETY.

Manadhata P., Wing J.(2005). An attack Surface Metric. *Carnegie Mellon University*Pittsburgh

Manadhata P. Jeanette P., Wing J.(2005). An attack Surface Metric. CMU-CS-155, School of Computer Science. *Carnegie Mellon University*Pittsburgh

Manske K.(2000). Amn Introduction to Social Engineering. Information Security Journal: A Global perspective 9:1-7

Matsumura M. Brauel B. And Shah J.(2009) SOA for Dummies. Software AG Special Edition Wiley publishing inc.

Mbuguah S.M.,Muketha G.M. Wabwoba F.(2014). A review of Algorithm for determination of Attackability Metrics. Journal of Emerging Trends in Computing and Information Science Vol.5. No 4

Mbuguah S.M.,Mwangi W. Song P.C. Muketha G.M.(2013). Experimental, Validation Of Technical attackability Metrics Model. International Journal of Information and Communication Technology Research. Vol.3. No 6

Mbuguah S.M.,Mwangi W. Song P.C. Muketha G.M.(2013). Social Attackability , Metrics for software systems. International Journal of Information and , Communication Technology Research. Vol.3. No 6

Mbuguah S.M.,Mwangi W. Song P.C. Muketha G.M.(2012). A Conceptual Model for a Holistic Predictive Attackability metrics for Secure Service Oriented Architecture Softwarre. International Journal of Information and Communication Technology Research. Vol.2. No 7

Melton A.C, Gustafson D. A. Bieman J.M. and Baker A.C (1990.). A mathematical perspective for software measures research. " *Software Eng. J., vol. 5, no. 5,* , , pp. 246-254,

Microsoft. (2010). *Security Bulletins.* , http://www.microsoft.com/technet/security/current.asp.

MITRE. (2010). *CVEs.* http://www.cve.mitre.org.

Mitnick, K.D., Simon W.L and Wozniak s.(2002) The Art Of Deception Controlling
,   the Human Element of Security. Indianapolis: Wiley

Mozilla Firefox,. (2009). Retrieved July 2009., from http://www.mozilla.com/en-.
    US/firefox

Muketha G.M.(2011) Size And Complexity Metrics as Indicators of Maintainability ,
    of Business Process Execution Language Process Models. PhD Thesis ,
    University Putra Malaysia

Myers G.J(1995). Reliable Software Through composite Design   Petrocelli Charter

Nandagam J. (1995) . A measure of Module Cohesion, *A dissertation University of ,*
,   *Southern Western Louisana*

Natis Y.V.(2003). Service Oriented Architecture Scenario. *Gartner Inc.*

Neuhaus S., Zulkerman.T. (2007,). "Predicting Vulnerable Software Components,"
    in the Proc. of the 14th ACM Conference on. *Computer and Communications ,*
    Security, (pp. pp. 529-540.). Virginia, USA,: ACM.

Nirebburg S. And Raskin V.(2004). Ontological Semantics. *Cambridge MA" MIT ,*
    Press.

Obrst L.(2007). Ontology and Ontologies:Why they matter to inlligence community.
In the Proceedings of the second ontology Semantics Conference Columbia 28-29

Olsson J(2004). Forensic Linguistics: An Introduction to Languages . *Crime And ,*
    Law New York.

Ortalo R.,Deswarte Y. Kaaniche M. (1999)., Experimenting with Quantitative ,
    Evaluation Tools for Monitoring Operational Security. *IEEE Transactions on ,*
    Software Engineering 25,5 (pp. p.633-650.). IEEE.

Pincus J. And Wing J.M.(2004). A template for Microsoft Security Bulletins in ,
    Terms of an Attack surface Model. *Report Microsoft research*

Raskin, V. Hempelmann, C. F., and Taylor J. M.(2010) Application-guided ,
    ontological engineering, In H.A. Arabnia,D. de la Fuente, E. B. Kozerenko, ,
    and J. A. Olivas. Eds. *Proceedings of International Conference on Artificial ,*
    Intelligence, Las Vegas, NE,

Raskin V., Attallah M.J, McDonough CJ. And Nirenburg S.(2001). Natural , Language Processing for Information Assurance and security. New Security . Paradigm *Workshop Ballycotton County Cork Ireland ACM press 51-65*

Rivlin and Gary (2006). Wallflower at the Web Party. *New York Times*

Saltzer J.and .Schroeder M. (1975). "The Protection of Information in Computer , Systems" . *Proc. of the IEEE 63 (9)* (pp. pp. 1278-1308,).

Scott V.B and McIntosh W.D.(1999) The Development of a trait measure of . ruminative thought Elsevier Science Ltd.

Shaffer Clifford A . Clifford A (2011)A Practical Introduction to Data Structures and Algorithm Analysis Edition 3.2 (Java Version) *Department of Computer , Science Virginia TechBlacksburg, VA 24061*

Shin Y. (2008). "Exploring Complexity Metrics as Indicators of Software , Vulnerability,". *in the 3rd International Doctoral Symposium onEmpirical , Software Engineering, ,* . Kaiserslautern, Germany.

Shin Y.and Williams L . (2008). "An Empirical Model to Predict Security , Vulnerabilities Using Code Complexity Metrics,. *2nd ACM-IEEE , International Symposium on Empirical Software Engineering and , Measurement,* (pp. pp. 315-317.). Kaiserslautern, Germany,: ACM-IEEE.

Shuy R.W.(2005) Creating Language crimes : How Law enforcement uses and , Misuses Language New York Oxford press

Smith B.(1995). Formal Ontology , Common Sense and cognitive science. , *International Journal of Human Computer Studies 43(5/6), 626-640*

Sowa J.F(2000). Knowledge Representation:Logical,Philosophical and , Computational foundation. *Pacific Grove. CA:Brooks/Cole*

Stevens S.J., Brllovin S.M.,Hershkop S. Keromytis A. Sinclair S. And Smith S.W. Eds(2008). *Insider attack and Cyber Security:Beyond the Hacker New York*

Stajano F. and Wilson P.(2009). Understanding Scam Victims: Seven Principles for , System Security. *Technical Report UCAM-CL-TR-754, University of , Cambridge UK*

Stamper CL. And Masteson S.(2002).How employee perception of insider threat , status affect their work Behaviour. Journal of Organization Behaviour 23 , . 873-894

Stewart & Neil(2009).IR magazine . Did CEO tweet violate quite Period Knocville , News Sentinel DOI

Stround K.A. (1993). Further Engineering Mathematics *Macmillan press*

Swiderski F. and Snyder W(2004). *Threat Modeling,.* Microsoft Press .

Taylor J.M. Raskin V.,Hempeilman C.F. and Attardo S.(2010). An Unintentional , inference and ontological property defaults.*In the Procedding of SMC 2010*

Thornburgh T.(2004). Social Engineering: the Dark Art: *In the proceddingof the 1ˢᵗ . conference on information curriculum development, GA, 133-135*

T''urpe .S and Eichler S.(2009). *Testing production Systems safely:Common . precautions in Penetration Testing. In proceeding of Testing Academic and , Industrial Conference(TAIC 2009) pg 205-209.IEEE & Computer Society*

T'onnis M.,Thompson L.K. and Lange C.(2006). Driver Visual Behaviour while , interacting with adaptive cruise control. *In the 50ᵗʰ Annual Meeting of Human Factors and Ergonomics Society(HFES)*

Voas J. (1996). Defining an Adaptive Software Security Metric from aDynamic , Software Failure Tolerance Measure, . *Proceedingsof the 11th Annual , Conference on Computer Assurance.*

Wayne, J. (2009). Directions in security Metrics Research. *National Institute Of , Standards and Technology USA Department Of Commerce.*

Weyuker E.J.(1998) Evaluating Software complexity measures, *IEEE transaction on , Software Engiineering 14:1358-1365*

Williams Y. S. (2008,). "Is Complexity Really the Enemy of Software Security?,*in , the Proc. of the 4th ACM Workshop on Quality of Protection,* (pp. pp. 47-50). , Virginia, USA: ACM.

Willison R. & Siponen M.(2009). Overcoming Insider threat:reducing employee , computer crime through situational crime prevention. *Communication of the , ACM 52(9) 133-137*

Wilson, F. S. (2011, march). Understanding Scam Victims:Seven Principles For , system Security. *Communication Of ACM, Vol 54,No3* .

Wing, P. M. (2004). *Measuring a System's Attack Surface, Technical Report CMU.* . Pittsburgh,: School of Computer Science, Carnegie Mellon University, .

Winkler I & Dealy B.(1995) Information Security Technology. Don't rely on it . A case Study in Social engineering. *In Proceeding of the 5th USENIX/UNIX . Symposium Salt Lake City Uta*

Yourdon E. And Constantine L.(1999). Structured Design. Fundamentals of a , Discipline of Computer Program and System design . Prentice Hall

144